Teen Addiction

OTHER BOOKS OF RELATED INTEREST

OPPOSING VIEWPOINTS SERIES
Addiction
Alcohol
Chemical Dependency
Drug Abuse
The Family
Teens at Risk
Tobacco and Smoking

CURRENT CONTROVERSIES SERIES
Alcoholism
Crime
Drug Trafficking
Illegal Drugs
Smoking
Teen Addiction
Teens and Alcohol

AT ISSUE SERIES
Heroin
Legalizing Drugs
Marijuana
Smoking

Teen
Addiction

Shasta Gaughen, *Book Editor*

Daniel Leone, *President*
Bonnie Szumski, *Publisher*
Scott Barbour, *Managing Editor*
Brenda Stalcup, *Series Editor*

Contemporary Issues
Companion

Greenhaven Press, Inc., San Diego, CA

Every effort has been made to trace the owners of copyrighted material. The articles in this volume may have been edited for content, length, and/or reading level. The titles have been changed to enhance the editorial purpose. Those interested in locating the original source will find the complete citation on the first page of each article.

Library of Congress Cataloging-in-Publication Data

Teen addiction / Shasta Gaughen, book editor.
    p. cm. — (Contemporary issues companion)
    Includes bibliographical references and index.
    ISBN 0-7377-0842-5 (pbk. : alk. paper) —
ISBN 0-7377-0843-3 (lib. : alk. paper)
    1. Teenagers—Substance use. 2. Substance abuse. 3. Compulsive behavior. I. Gaughen, Shasta. II. Series.

HV4999.Y68 T45 2002
362.29'0835'1—dc21   2001040781
                                                                      CIP

© 2002 by Greenhaven Press, Inc.
10911 Technology Place, San Diego, CA 92127

Printed in the U.S.A.

CONTENTS

FOREWORD

In the news, on the streets, and in neighborhoods, individuals are confronted with a variety of social problems. Such problems may affect people directly: A young woman may struggle with depression, suspect a friend of having bulimia, or watch a loved one battle cancer. And even the issues that do not directly affect her private life—such as religious cults, domestic violence, or legalized gambling—still impact the larger society in which she lives. Discovering and analyzing the complexities of issues that encompass communal and societal realms as well as the world of personal experience is a valuable educational goal in the modern world.

Effectively addressing social problems requires familiarity with a constantly changing stream of data. Becoming well informed about today's controversies is an intricate process that often involves reading myriad primary and secondary sources, analyzing political debates, weighing various experts' opinions—even listening to first-hand accounts of those directly affected by the issue. For students and general observers, this can be a daunting task because of the sheer volume of information available in books, periodicals, on the evening news, and on the Internet. Researching the consequences of legalized gambling, for example, might entail sifting through congressional testimony on gambling's societal effects, examining private studies on Indian gaming, perusing numerous websites devoted to Internet betting, and reading essays written by lottery winners as well as interviews with recovering compulsive gamblers. Obtaining valuable information can be time-consuming—since it often requires researchers to pore over numerous documents and commentaries before discovering a source relevant to their particular investigation.

Greenhaven's Contemporary Issues Companion series seeks to assist this process of research by providing readers with useful and pertinent information about today's complex issues. Each volume in this anthology series focuses on a topic of current interest, presenting informative and thought-provoking selections written from a wide variety of viewpoints. The readings selected by the editors include such diverse sources as personal accounts and case studies, pertinent factual and statistical articles, and relevant commentaries and overviews. This diversity of sources and views, found in every Contemporary Issues Companion, offers readers a broad perspective in one convenient volume.

In addition, each title in the Contemporary Issues Companion series is designed especially for young adults. The selections included in every volume are chosen for their accessibility and are expertly edited in consideration of both the reading and comprehension levels of the audience. The structure of the anthologies also enhances accessibility. An introductory essay places each issue in context and provides helpful facts such as historical background or current statistics and legislation that pertain to the topic. The chapters that follow organize the material and focus on specific aspects of the book's topic. Every essay is introduced by a brief summary of its main points and biographical information about the author. These summaries aid in comprehension and can also serve to direct readers to material of immediate interest and need. Finally, a comprehensive index allows readers to efficiently scan and locate content.

The Contemporary Issues Companion series is an ideal launching point for research on a particular topic. Each anthology in the series is composed of readings taken from an extensive gamut of resources, including periodicals, newspapers, books, government documents, the publications of private and public organizations, and Internet websites. In these volumes, readers will find factual support suitable for use in reports, debates, speeches, and research papers. The anthologies also facilitate further research, featuring a book and periodical bibliography and a list of organizations to contact for additional information.

A perfect resource for both students and the general reader, Greenhaven's Contemporary Issues Companion series is sure to be a valued source of current, readable information on social problems that interest young adults. It is the editors' hope that readers will find the Contemporary Issues Companion series useful as a starting point to formulate their own opinions about and answers to the complex issues of the present day.

INTRODUCTION

The use of mind-altering substances has long been an important part of rituals for cultures all over the world. In particular, the consumption of plant-based hallucinogens is frequently found in ceremonies that deal with the transition from childhood to adulthood. In southern California, for example, one rite of passage for young Native American boys involved the ceremonial consumption of a special drink made from a plant called *toloache*, which contains compounds that cause hallucinations. These hallucinations were a crucial part of the ceremony in which the boys were guided by tribal shamans into adulthood. Even in the present day, religious ceremonies involving children and teens may entail the ritualized consumption of alcohol, as in the celebration of First Communion in Catholicism. Clearly, the use of such substances in socially sanctioned rites of passage has a long history in most societies.

Some teens today appear to consider their personal use of drugs, tobacco, and alcohol as a sort of rite of passage, marking their entrance into adulthood. Like the Native American youth of long ago in southern California, these teens may view the use of such substances as a way of transitioning into a world of adult behaviors. However, contemporary teens' personal use of these substances differs dramatically from that seen in traditional cultures or mainstream religions. The major difference is that these teens use tobacco, alcohol, and drugs repeatedly, without adult supervision or permission, and they often become addicted.

What are the causes of teen addiction? This question has been addressed by many scientists and researchers, and although there are no definite answers yet, several facts have become evident. Researchers have established that there are a variety of reasons why a teenager will begin experimenting with—and possibly become addicted to—drugs, alcohol, tobacco, or even gambling. A report released in February 2001 by the National Center on Addiction and Substance Abuse (CASA) at Columbia University in New York found that up to 61 percent of teenagers are at risk for substance abuse. Teens included in the survey identified drugs as the most important problem they face. Joseph A. Califano Jr., chairman of the center, stressed that children with "hands-on" parents who set clear rules and keep strict tabs on their kids' activities, friends, and whereabouts are far less likely to become substance abusers—but only 27 percent of the teens surveyed for the report had such parents. However, the CASA report found that even children with highly involved parents are still at risk for substance abuse, facing half the average risk of teens with "hands-off" parents.

Obviously, parental involvement is only one part of the equation that determines which teens will become addicted. According to the American Academy of Pediatrics (AAP), genetic and family factors play an important role. Teens who have a family history of alcohol or substance abuse run an increased risk of become addicts themselves— even if they are not raised by their birth family—which points to the possibility that genetic factors predispose certain individuals to addiction. Furthermore, teens who grow up in a home environment filled with substance abuse are placed at great risk for addiction. Parents who abuse drugs and alcohol generally have poor parenting skills, the AAP states, and they pass these negative and self-destructive behaviors on to their children. Older siblings also have a strong influence; the desire to be "cool" like an older brother or sister can lead teens to indulge in excessive drinking, smoking, or drug use. Similarly, pressure from friends or the desire to emulate "cool" peers can cause teenagers to experiment with these substances.

Social attitudes are also an essential factor behind teen addiction. Movies, television, music, and advertising often portray the use of alcohol, tobacco, and drugs as sophisticated and commonplace. In particular, youths receive mixed messages about drinking, smoking, and gambling since these activities are legal for adults, yet illegal for minors. Nikki Babbit, a psychologist and therapist who specializes in treating young addicts and their families, writes in her book *Adolescent Drug and Alcohol Abuse* that "adolescents are living in a drug culture that never existed before. Alcohol continues to be the most easily abused drug because of its availability and the fact that it is socially sanctioned." The problem of teen addiction is further exacerbated by the sense of immortality that many youths feel. As Babbit asserts, "Adolescents think they are invincible. They are aware that there are potential dangers when they use drugs or binge on alcohol, but think they will escape them."

Another factor behind teen substance abuse, recently discovered by scientists, is that the use of alcohol and drugs by adolescents has a different effect on them physically and psychologically than it does on adults, making them more prone to addiction. Adolescents' brains are still developing physically, and scientific research has revealed that their brains are consequently more receptive to the effects of drugs and alcohol than are adult brains. Specifically, adolescent brains develop more powerful receptors to addictive substances, which may accelerate the rate at which teens become addicted. Scientists have also found that excessive use of alcohol by teens may lead to brain damage, particularly in the parts of the brain associated with addiction. Because teens' brains are not fully mature, they have yet to develop the same abilities as adults for assessing risks, including those involved in using alcohol, drugs, and tobacco. In addition, the unique psychological stresses of adolescence can cause teens who are already at risk for substance abuse to become even more likely to try using alcohol or drugs to block out their problems.

While the causes of teen addiction are still not completely understood, there is no doubt that substance abuse by teens has been a problem for a long time. Teens have used and abused a wide variety of substances over the years, often in search of a new or better high. Currently, the popularity of some drugs seems to be declining, while the use of others is steady or on the rise. The annual Monitoring the Future survey, conducted by the University of Michigan Institute for Social Research in Ann Arbor, measures the use of drugs, alcohol, and tobacco among eighth, tenth, and twelfth graders in the United States. In 2000, the survey found that the use of several drugs—including inhalants, LSD, crystal methamphetamine, and Rohypnol—has declined significantly among teens in recent years since reaching a peak in 1996. In addition, the results of the survey indicated considerable decreases in the use of heroin, crack and powder cocaine, and cigarettes and chewing tobacco.

Although these findings are good news, the survey also uncovered several discouraging facts. For instance, it revealed that teenagers' use of certain drugs—such as amphetamines, barbiturates, tranquilizers, non-LSD hallucinogens, opiates, and alcohol—has remained unchanged. Furthermore, while the popularity of some "traditional" drugs seems to be declining, new drugs are quickly taking their place. The most rapidly growing drug in this category is ecstasy. Ecstasy is the popular name for the drug methylenedioxymethamphetamine (MDMA), which is both a stimulant and a hallucinogen. This drug is most commonly used by young people attending all-night dance parties called raves, who take ecstasy to enhance the experience of beat-heavy club music and dancing. The Monitoring the Future survey for the year 2000 discovered that the use of ecstasy has not just grown substantially among tenth and twelfth graders, but has also reached eighth graders for the first time.

Because ecstasy is commonly touted as a "natural" drug, many teens are unaware that it can have drastic, sometimes fatal, consequences. A February 2001 article in the journal *Science World* notes that there were sixty-eight ecstasy-related emergency room visits in 1993; by 1997, that number had jumped to 637, a nearly tenfold increase. The problems associated with ecstasy include strokes, seizures, and severe dehydration. One young teen reports that she took ecstasy to overcome her feelings of shyness and insecurity, but once the drug wore off, she suddenly faced new problems: an inability to concentrate, depression, and difficulty speaking clearly. Another teen ecstasy user, a young man of sixteen, ingested a fatal overdose of the drug and was found dead in Madison, Wisconsin, the day after a rave.

In spite of the dangers of ecstasy use, teen consumption of the drug continues to escalate. Customs agents expect to seize seven to eight million pills entering the United States in 2001. Research scientist Lloyd D. Johnston, who works on the Monitoring the Future project, compares the use of ecstasy today to cocaine in the late 1970s and early 1980s. He explains that during this time period, most young people were not fully aware of the harmful effects or the addictive nature of cocaine and therefore were more willing to experiment with the drug than they might otherwise have been. "Maybe this generation of young people could learn from that earlier generation's mistake by learning not to trust all those reassuring things they hear about the newest drug on the block—in this case, ecstasy," Johnston states.

Despite all the messages teens receive about the dangers of addiction, many will be tempted to try alcohol, tobacco, drugs, or gambling, and some will become addicted. As long as the problem of teen addiction exists, researchers will continue to search for answers to the questions of why and how teens become addicted and to explore possible avenues for cures to teen addiction. The authors included in *Teen Addiction: Contemporary Issues Companion* address these vital issues, and present an examination of the nature and scope of various types of teen addiction. Rounding out this anthology are teenagers' personal accounts of their own struggles with addiction and their progress toward recovery. Taken as a whole, the diverse selections collected in these pages offer a timely and pertinent overview of the serious issue of teen addiction.

CHAPTER 1

THE PROBLEM OF TEEN ADDICTION: AN OVERVIEW

The Physical Effects of Addiction

Melissa Abramovitz

Teenagers who use drugs and alcohol do not intend to become addicted. Nevertheless, as Melissa Abramovitz writes in the following article, they are unable to avoid the chemical effects of drugs—including alcohol and tobacco—on their brains and bodies. Many drugs create both psychological and physical dependence, she explains, and teens can experience serious withdrawal symptoms when they try to stop taking these drugs. Additionally, as the body begins to tolerate the effects of the drugs, the user needs to take increasingly larger doses to achieve a high, often with life-threatening results. The author also notes that teens seem to be particularly susceptible to addiction because young people are more sensitive to the effects of drugs. Abramovitz is a freelance writer who contributes to a variety of national and local publications.

Charlie had no intention of getting addicted. "I just liked getting high," the 16-year-old says. "I forgot about my problems when I was high."

He started with a few alcoholic drinks at a party, but within a year, he was drinking almost every day. If he didn't drink, he got jittery, headachy, and nauseated.

Then his friend Travis told him about "crank" (methamphetamine). "You have so much energy," Travis boasted. "You can stay up all night."

So Charlie snorted crank. At first, he felt energetic, as Travis promised. But after several months, he realized he needed the drug. He dreaded the crash into depression when the drug wore off. So he started stealing money from his parents to keep buying more. He lost weight and started failing his classes in school. But he didn't seem to care about anything except getting more drugs.

The Power of Addiction

Even though Charlie had no intention of becoming addicted to drugs, these chemical powerhouses took over his life. Once he made the deci-

sion to start taking crank—a psychoactive, or mind-altering, substance—
he eventually lost his ability to say no. Psychoactive drugs change the
way the brain works. Over time, these brain changes make the user's
mind and body need more and more of the drug.

Many addicts develop both psychological and physical addiction,
or dependence. With psychological addiction, the person craves the
drug to achieve certain effects, like an improved mood. With physical dependence, the body goes through withdrawal if use of the drug
is discontinued.

Typical withdrawal symptoms include nausea, chills, sweating,
anxiety, headaches, and sometimes convulsions. Charlie experienced
some of these symptoms after not taking alcohol or crank for about
eight hours. Some addicts get such severe withdrawal symptoms, they
have to be hospitalized.

Tolerance is another aspect of physical dependence. The brain and
body get used to a drug. Eventually, the user needs more and more to
get the same effect. Sometimes the dose required to bring on a high is
so large, it becomes life-threatening.

Drug Dependency

Besides alcohol and crank, teens become addicted to a variety of legal
and illegal drugs each year. Illegal drugs are especially dangerous,
because the people who prepare and sell them sometimes mix them
with fillers like Drano that are poisonous.

Young people are more susceptible to a drug's effects than are
adults. So how quickly someone becomes addicted often depends on
the person's age. The speed with which addiction is brought on also
depends on the particular drug, how much a person takes, and how
it's taken. Drugs that are snorted, smoked, or injected reach the brain
almost immediately and tend to produce addiction quickest.

Depressant drugs slow down the nervous system and make the user
feel sleepy. They include alcohol—legal for adults over 21 but illegal
for teens—barbiturates (sleeping pills), tranquilizers (nerve calmers),
and inhalants like glue and paint thinner.

Besides being highly addictive and producing tolerance, many of
these drugs can cause serious liver diseases. It's also easy to overdose
and even die from them. Some teens who sniff glue, for example,
develop tolerance to the point where they need several tubes to get
high. This can result in hospitalization or death.

Stimulants rev up the mind and body, increasing alertness, heart
rate, blood pressure, and body temperature. They cause sleeplessness,
runny nose, and decreased appetite. And some can produce an
intense feeling of euphoria or pleasure. They can cause heart attacks
or brain seizures and are highly addictive.

Nicotine, the stimulant in tobacco, is extremely addictive, as smokers who try to quit are very aware. Amphetamine and methampheta-

mine (speed and crank) are used as diet pills and energy boosters and are highly addictive.

Cocaine and crack act quickly and directly on the brain's pleasure centers. These drugs can be snorted, smoked, or injected. Even a single dose can cause heart failure and death. . . . Caffeine, the stimulant drug found in colas, coffee, tea, and chocolate, is a widely used legal stimulant. Like other "uppers," caffeine creates tolerance, dependence, and withdrawal symptoms such as fatigue, headache, and depression.

Opiates, or narcotics, make people dreamy and sleepy and are strongly addictive. They include morphine, heroin, and similar pain relievers. Heroin is the most abused illegal narcotic. Because it's often injected, addicts who use shared or dirty needles can get diseases such as AIDS and hepatitis.

Marijuana produces relaxation, fuzzy thinking, and lack of coordination, along with increased heart rate and red eyes. It is mostly psychologically addictive, though long-term users go through physical withdrawal.

Hallucinogens like LSD (acid) and PCP (angel dust) alter thinking and moods and are psychologically addictive. Because their effects are unpredictable, they are dangerous. They often lead to frightening hallucinations, serious injuries, and convulsions.

The Chemical Forces Behind Addiction

Doctors used to think that people addicted to drugs were "weak" or simply didn't want to quit. But new technology now allows doctors to see how addictive drugs change the brain. Most doctors now agree that addiction is a disease, not a weakness.

PET (positron emission tomography) and SPECT (single photon emission computed tomography) machines allow researchers to watch what happens in the brain during a drug "high" and a withdrawal. Addictive drugs act on neurotransmitters, the chemical messengers in the brain, changing the amount of these chemicals or their response.

PET and SPECT scans, for example, show that cocaine causes brain cells to release large amounts of the chemical dopamine, along with other neurotransmitters. Dopamine causes a feeling of euphoria. When the drug wears off, the sudden drop in dopamine contributes to the "crash" of withdrawal.

Alcohol creates changes in brain levels of the neurotransmitters norepinephrine, serotonin, and glutamate. Too much glutamate is known to poison and kill brain cells. This helps explain why it's so powerfully addictive and also why alcoholics may show severe brain damage.

Besides helping scientists understand the hows and whys of addiction, the study of brain chemistry helps doctors search for new ways of treating drug dependence. A couple of new treatments are being worked on—one to prevent cocaine addiction and another to help alcoholics stop craving alcohol.

Other forces besides neurotransmitters push people toward drug addiction. Genetic factors that affect how the brain responds to drugs play a big part, experts say. Researchers have found several genes linked to nicotine, cocaine, and alcohol addiction. And they find that people who become addicted to one drug are very likely to develop an addiction to other drugs as well.

Of course, genes aren't the whole story. Not everyone with an addictive gene becomes an addict. People who never start drinking can't become alcoholic.

So other factors, such as family habits, are also important influences. When teens see their parents or other family members drinking or taking drugs to cope, they may be influenced to do the same. Drug use among friends also is a big factor in shaping addictive behavior. A report by the National Institutes of Health showed that teens who begin drinking alcohol with their friends before age 15 are four times likelier to become alcoholic than are people who wait until age 21 to drink.

Avoiding Addiction

Addiction is a trap, whether it's triggered by family habits, pressure from friends, or a desire to get high. Before you let yourself fall into the addiction trap, remember that these drugs cause brain changes that are very hard to undo. The only sure way to avoid the problems that drug addiction brings is to not start in the first place.

Kicking a nicotine or alcohol or cocaine habit is incredibly difficult. In Charlie's words, "When I finally tried to get alcohol and crank out of my life, it was the hardest thing I've ever done. I was in therapy for six months. But I had to do it, since the drugs were killing me. I had to get my life back."

THE CONSEQUENCES OF USING TOBACCO, ALCOHOL, AND MARIJUANA

Kathiann M. Kowalski

Teens are often tempted into trying cigarettes, chewing tobacco, alcohol, and marijuana before they are aware of the consequences. As freelance writer Kathiann M. Kowalski points out in the following selection, use of any of these substances can lead to addiction and serious health problems. There is also substantial evidence that teens who use these substances are more likely to try stronger drugs, she explains. Despite media messages that portray the use of tobacco, alcohol, and marijuana as "cool," Kowalski maintains, teens who use these substances put themselves and those around them at risk. In addition, she states, use of these substances can lead to teens becoming alienated from family and friends, being expelled from school, getting fired from jobs, or even doing jail time.

Devon started drinking at a friend's house at age 11. Soon, she was using marijuana, cocaine, and "whatever I could get my hands on." Before turning 16, Devon had been arrested twice for underage drinking and marijuana use. Eventually, an overdose of alcohol and cocaine landed the Minnesota teen in a hospital.

Almost everyone who uses cocaine, heroin, and other drugs starts with tobacco, alcohol, or marijuana. In their 1998 Monitoring the Future Study, University of Michigan researchers asked teens what drugs they had used during the previous month. Among 12th graders, 35 percent said they had smoked cigarettes, 52 percent had drunk alcohol, and 23 percent had used marijuana. Misled by billions of dollars in advertising and images in movies, experts say, teens often don't realize where these substances can lead.

The Negative Effects of Tobacco Use

Despite health warnings on each cigarette pack, about 3,000 young people start smoking every day. The Centers for Disease Control and

Prevention (CDC), a U.S. government agency, says roughly 1,000 of them will become addicted to nicotine, one of tobacco's approximately 4,000 chemicals. Before turning 18, 70 percent of teen smokers regret starting. Yet many will remain addicted until they become ill with tobacco-related diseases.

Tobacco companies need young smokers. More than 400,000 Americans die each year from tobacco-related illnesses. These include lung cancer, chronic bronchitis, emphysema, heart attacks, high blood pressure, strokes, and arteriosclerosis (hardening of the arteries). Chewers risk cancers of the esophagus, mouth, and throat, and loss of teeth.

But teens don't have to wait decades to get sick from tobacco. Smoking reduces lung capacity soon after a person starts, causing shortness of breath and reduced stamina. That's bad for playing sports or even just climbing stairs between classes. Smokers suffer more from asthma, as well as colds, pneumonia, flu, and other infections. Add stained teeth and fingers, foul breath, and smelly clothes. No wonder most teens prefer dating nonsmokers.

And with all that negative stuff, no wonder the tobacco industry spends billions each year on advertising. Despite ads' attempts at "grown-up" images, few people start smoking after age 18. As a 1981 document by tobacco company Philip Morris said, "Today's teenager is tomorrow's potential regular customer."

Do you doubt the power of advertising on teens? The Campaign for Tobacco-Free Kids says 86 percent of youth smokers prefer Marlboro, Camel, and Newport, the three most advertised brands. Only one-third of adult smokers prefer those brands.

Even with the tobacco industry's billions of dollars in advertising, Florida's anti-tobacco stance has seen recent downturns in teen smoking rates. Teens in Florida have been clued in. Activist Christina Scelsi, age 17, credits a campaign to expose the tobacco industry by SWAT—Students Working Against Tobacco. "It encourages teens to positively rebel by not smoking and not letting the tobacco industry take them in and addict them to nicotine," says Christina.

Alcohol—Not as Advertised

Like tobacco, alcohol is readily available to teens. Beavers and bar scenes in TV ads make alcohol seem fun. But for Keith Noble, Steven Donnelly, and Scott Krueger, alcohol was a killer. Many other teens have shared these college honor students' fate. Fifty college students die each year after "binge drinking"—consuming five drinks in a row for males or four for females.

Alcohol is illegal in every state for people under age 21. Yet 25 percent of eighth graders in the Monitoring the Future Study already had gotten drunk. For 12th graders, the figure was 62 percent.

Alcohol acts as a depressant in the body. It depresses, or slows down, the central nervous system, affecting judgment and coordination.

Alicia became aware of this effect early on. She began drinking when she was 15. Over time, Alicia grew to hate the out-of-control feeling she got from alcohol's blur. Now the Ohio teen no longer drinks alcohol. "I was not really big on drinking to get drunk, and a lot of people were," Alicia says. "Why would I do something so I wouldn't be in control?"

People react to alcohol differently. One drink relaxes many people. Two or three can make some people lose their inhibitions. Four or five can cause aggression.

On college campuses, most fights, property destruction, date rapes, sexually transmitted diseases, unwanted pregnancies, and accidents have some link to alcohol. Even if teens don't become violent themselves, drinking makes them more vulnerable to attacks. Devon, for example, was at a drinking party when she was attacked and raped.

Alcohol use—by the victim, the perpetrator, or both—is implicated in 46 to 75 percent of date rapes of college students, according to a report by the National Center on Addiction and Substance Abuse (CASA) at Columbia University.

Sadly, people under alcohol's influence often don't realize it. "I felt like there was never an amount of alcohol that was too much for me," Jonathan recalls. After drinking all night, Jonathan crashed his car and killed his 18-year-old friend Justin. Jonathan wound up doing prison time in Georgia for vehicular homicide and driving under the influence.

The more a person drinks, the higher his or her blood alcohol concentration (BAC) is. Alcohol's absorption into the body depends on gender, weight, and various other factors. In many states, an adult over 21 is legally drunk if his or her BAC is 0.8 or above. Some states have a limit of 0.5.

Despite these numbers, even a single drink impairs the rapid-fire responses needed for safe driving. Generally, exceeding any detectable BAC—0.02 or less—is illegal for all drivers under age 21.

Beyond its immediate effects, alcohol can cause anemia, sleep disorders, liver disease, heart disease, damage to the esophagus and pancreas, and cancer. Alcohol abuse also can have a detrimental effect on school performance and personal relationships.

Of course, none of these effects show up in ads for beer or other alcoholic beverages. After all, how much alcohol would people buy if they saw ruined lives instead of smart-aleck lizards?

Marijuana Is a Dangerous Drug

Alcohol and tobacco are legal drugs for adults, and they are easily available. But another drug, marijuana, is illegal for everyone. Yet it's accessible to everyone—adults and teens.

Marijuana goes by many names: pot, grass, reefer, roach, smoke, dope, joint, Mary Jane, and others. Because marijuana is illegal, it's not advertised directly. But at least a half-dozen movies in 1999 portrayed marijuana as cool. Real life is nothing like the movie hype.

Derived from a hemp plant called *Cannabis sativa*, marijuana contains hundreds of chemicals. A main ingredient responsible for marijuana's "high" is delta-9-tetrahydrocannabinol, or THC.

Most people who smoke or eat marijuana want to get "high." Some users feel relaxed or detached. Others get giddy or silly. But marijuana's health effects are anything but silly.

Marijuana is at least as bad for your lungs as tobacco. Smoking marijuana can cause lung cancer and other respiratory diseases. It causes temporary increases in heart rate. And it can affect the immune system—the body's defenses against disease.

Beyond this, marijuana affects the brain. Studies of college students showed decreased ability to concentrate and remember things. Even after highs wore off, marijuana users consistently scored lower on various tests. With college admissions or job interviews ahead, the last thing any teen needs is something that interferes with memory, reasoning, and even understanding simple ideas. Marijuana also blunts coordination and concentration, making driving, sports, and other activities very dangerous.

Marijuana alters users' moods. Even if a user avoids paranoia and hallucinations, marijuana's "high" hinders good judgment. "That puts you at risk for making poor life decisions," stresses Alan Leshner, director of the National Institute on Drug Abuse (NIDA). Unprotected sexual activity (with risks of AIDS and sexually transmitted infections), use of other drugs, and impaired driving are just a few dangerous behaviors that correlate with marijuana use.

As if that's not enough, marijuana is illegal. Getting high isn't worth the risk of jail time, a huge fine, and a criminal record. Nor is it worth the risk of getting knocked off a sports team or being rejected for a job. Since traces remain in the body for a long time, many schools and businesses use testing to screen out people who use marijuana and other drugs.

In 1999 CASA announced that more teens and children entered treatment for marijuana abuse than for all other drugs—more than 87,000 in 1996. Movie makers wouldn't pull in such huge profits if they replaced silly stoned characters with real-life suffering teens.

Opening the Door to Other Addictions?

Why do so many teens keep using tobacco, alcohol, and marijuana? And might they lead to use of other drugs?

"The truth is, if you don't use alcohol, tobacco, or marijuana by the time you're 21, the probability of ever becoming addicted to anything is virtually zero or is tremendously reduced," says NIDA's Leshner. "And the earlier you use substances, the greater the probability of becoming addicted to other things."

It's not necessarily a direct causal connection, notes Leshner. For example, many teens addicted to nicotine, alcohol, or marijuana have other emotional and psychological problems. Those problems, genetics, or other factors could explain the high correlation.

Nonetheless, the statistics are startling. "Among teens who report no other problem behaviors, those who used cigarettes, alcohol, and marijuana at least once in the past month are almost 17 times likelier to use another drug like cocaine, heroin, or LSD," says CASA's president, Joseph A. Califano, Jr.

How are these drugs linked to harder drugs? Important clues lie in how nicotine, alcohol, and THC affect the brain. At first the substances produce pleasant feelings. The body's response reinforces, or rewards, continued use. Over time, users develop a tolerance. They need more and more to get the same feeling. Soon, users become addicted to the substance.

Nicotine, for example, travels to the brain within 8 seconds. There it mimics effects of a neurotransmitter called acetylcholine. Neurotransmitters travel from nerve cell to nerve cell and cause responses. Acetylcholine affects muscle movement, breathing, heart rate, learning, memory, and hormone levels.

Nicotine also affects levels of another neurotransmitter called dopamine, which is associated with feelings of pleasure and reward. The pleasant feelings encourage the smoker to use tobacco again. Alcohol and marijuana likewise affect levels of dopamine and other neurotransmitters.

Cocaine, heroin, and other drugs also change levels of dopamine and other chemicals in the brain. These changes in brain chemistry suggest a link between tobacco, alcohol, and marijuana and other drugs. "While scientists have not yet discovered the smoking gun," says Califano, "they have certainly found the trigger finger."

"Adolescence is a particularly important period of life because of all the social, emotional, and physical development going on," notes Harvard Medical School's Elena Kouri. Beyond their effects on thinking and emotional functions, drugs can interfere with teens' motivation to develop to their full potential. "All drugs that have reinforcing properties (the ones that make you feel good) have the potential to become addictive," says Kouri. "Every time a person uses a drug or alcohol, the likelihood of the person becoming addicted to it increases."

Going Through Withdrawal

Addiction becomes harder to escape when withdrawal symptoms mount. Cigarette smokers feel restless, hungry, depressed, or suffer headaches. Problem drinkers get shaky, anxious, nauseous, and sweaty when they can't drink.

With heavy marijuana use, "the withdrawal syndrome is subtle, and oftentimes individuals don't associate it with marijuana," says Kouri. "Instead, they feel cranky, irritable, a little anxious." Even if withdrawal doesn't interfere with daily activities, Kouri says, "it is often severe enough to drive individuals to smoke marijuana again."

Hormones associated with the withdrawal response might make some teens crave something stronger. Or, while they're drunk or stoned, teens may experiment with other drugs. But it's a delusion for anyone to think they can control their use of addictive substances.

"The determinant of whether you become addicted is unknown," stresses NIDA's Leshner. Genetics, for example, may make you vulnerable without your knowing it. "Therefore, nobody is immune . . . and you need to protect yourself from the risks."

Far-Reaching Effects

Tobacco, alcohol, and marijuana don't affect just the people who use them. They affect family members and all the people with whom users come in contact. "A lot of my family members smoke," says 14-year-old Brittany from Runnemede, New Jersey, "and I have a hard time because I have asthma." Secondhand smoke also leads to other lung problems and increased infections.

Tobacco, alcohol, and marijuana strain relationships. Users may lie about use, steal from family members to support their habit, or become abusive to people they should love and trust.

Strangers get hurt too. Driving under the influence of alcohol or marijuana kills and injures thousands each year. And all of society suffers from the costs of higher health care expenses, destruction from violence, and lost opportunities from what users might have achieved.

Teens face enough challenges without the health hazards of tobacco, alcohol, and marijuana. "Nobody thinks they're going to get addicted. Nobody thinks they're going to get in trouble," says Alyse Booth, CASA's director of communications. "But on the other hand, why take the risk if you really value yourself and your future?"

ALCOHOL: THE DRUG OF CHOICE AMONG TEENS

Elizabeth Shepard

In the following article, Elizabeth Shepard maintains that the foremost drug problem among youth in the United States is alcohol. The adolescent brain is especially susceptible to alcohol's effects, Shepard points out, making teen drinkers more prone to alcoholism than people who begin drinking later in life. Parents, society, and the media send mixed messages to teens about the acceptability of drinking, she writes, which also contributes to the high rate of teen addiction to alcohol. In addition, Shepard contends, underage drinkers find it easy to gain access to alcohol, which exacerbates the problem and can lead to devastating accidents when drunk teens get behind the driver's wheel. Shepard is a freelance journalist and novelist.

Eighteen-year-old Leah Bean gave up alcohol in 1998. During her junior year in high school, Leah's best friend, April, was killed in a crash after leaving a party where kids had been drinking. The 19-year-old driver with whom April was riding crashed the car while driving with a blood alcohol content of .20 percent—more than twice the legal adult limit in Tennessee. According to Leah, the teens knew that party-goers were drinking and that the store which sold the teens alcohol was notorious for not checking IDs. But Leah echoes other teens' feelings of invincibility, admitting it is "as if there's a bubble around 15- to 21-year-olds that prevents bad things from happening."

Leah represents thousands of teenagers whose lives have been devastated by underage drinking. According to Monitoring the Future, a survey conducted by the University of Michigan, 31 percent of 12th-graders reported binge drinking (five or more drinks in a row) in the two weeks prior to the survey. Fifty-one percent reported consuming alcohol. Of eighth-graders, 15 percent reported binge drinking—and 24 percent consumed alcohol.

Parents' Role

Many parents allow their teenage children to drink alcohol at home in an effort to teach them how to drink responsibly. They may have good intentions, but the results can be deadly. What they do, in fact, is facilitate their kids' comfort with alcohol, and the trouble only begins there. . . .

"Kids don't know where to draw the line," Leah explained. "When parents open the door to alcohol for their kids, their kids figure if it's OK to drink at home, it's OK to drink out, too."

Many parents would be shocked to learn how young their children are when they begin to drink. Youth tend to begin drinking alcohol when they're as young as 12 years old. A recent study shows a four-in-one chance that kids who begin drinking at 13 will become problem drinkers—and most likely impaired drivers—as opposed to young people who don't drink until the age of 21. By the time teenagers get to college, their rate of consumption has escalated dramatically: 4.4 million of them are binge drinkers and another 1.8 million are heavy drinkers (consuming five or more drinks on one occasion at least five times in the past month).

In some cases, parents aren't even aware that the underage and excessive drinking is taking place. A good example is spring break. Many parents send their kids off on trips to relax and play in the sun. Most often, these vacations are weeklong drinking junkets or "booze cruises" with excessive alcohol consumption.

At the other extreme, parents sometimes acknowledge the drinking and help their teens plan parties hoping to ensure their safety by "controlling" their drinking environment. This was the case for teens from Highland Park, a wealthy Dallas suburb. Police broke up a warehouse party in Dallas and found that parents had rented the facility and contracted a bus company to safely deliver drunken high school students to and from the party.

But no matter how challenging parents may feel it is to communicate with their kids about alcohol, talking to them and setting clear boundaries are the most important things they can do. Survey after survey shows that young people rank parents among the top reasons for not using alcohol, demonstrating that parents have a great deal of impact and influence on their child's decision on whether to drink.

Laws holding parents liable for underage drinking incidents are becoming more common. It is evident that young people alone are not at the root of the underage drinking issue—adults often facilitate youth drinking by providing or buying the drinks.

Alcohol Is Everywhere

In 1998, about 10.4 million drinkers in the United States were less than 21 years old. Sure, it's illegal, but that doesn't mean kids can't get their hands on alcohol.

In fact, 75 percent of young teens say that alcohol is easy to acquire. Approximately two-thirds of teenagers who drink report that they buy their own alcohol. Whether they buy it from stores or at bars that sell without carding, from home delivery services improperly monitored by state laws or from friends and siblings, alcohol is everywhere and easily within youths' reach.

The Lawrence County, Tennessee, Mothers Against Drunk Driving (MADD) Youth In Action team conducted a study to see how many merchants sold alcohol to minors. Young men and women who were at least 21 years old but looked younger were sent into stores to try to purchase alcohol. The results were shocking: 48 percent of all salespeople never asked to see the buyers' identification. Of those sellers who asked, 50 percent of them sold the alcohol even after the buyers said they had no ID.

And it seems that underage drinkers make alcohol a priority in their budgets. Each year, college students spend approximately $5.5 billion on alcohol—more than they spend on soft drinks, milk, tea, coffee and books combined.

One 19-year-old college student, who wished to remain anonymous, said, "The drinking starts on Thursday nights and continues throughout the weekend. When one party runs out of alcohol, we all move on to another party. We drink until we can't drink another shot. Kids keep count of how many drinks they have each night; it's like a contest. When my parents send me my monthly check for living expenses, I make sure I save enough money to buy beer."

Teresa Robinson's 21-year-old daughter, Nicole, a college student, was killed in an alcohol-related crash November 13, 1997. "A group of kids went to a bar near campus to celebrate someone's 21st birthday, and they proceeded to get extremely drunk. Everyone at the bar knew that the kids were underage and drunk, but no one stopped them. The bartenders just kept serving everyone more drinks. I was stunned that no one in the bar tried to prevent the kids from getting in their cars."

Nicole was intoxicated when she got into the car being driven by a girl who was so drunk she fell on her face at the bar in front of the bartenders. The driver, with a blood alcohol content of .24 percent, was driving nearly 100 miles per hour when she crashed into a tree. The driver lived. Nicole died at the scene of the crash.

Teresa and her husband had cautioned Nicole never to drink and drive, and they never consumed any alcohol in front of their kids. "We were very conscientious about teaching our children about the dangers of alcohol. But I don't know how to get kids to listen. The media glorifies alcohol. The commercials are enticing. When kids get to college, it's a free-for-all—no one's watching them or saying yes or no. Kids who attended Nicole's funeral still drink and party and drive!"

The Media's Mixed Messages

Even parents who set good examples and have discussed the rules regarding alcohol use have a tough battle. Advertisers—which spend more than $1 billion each year on alcohol advertisements alone—still portray alcohol as alluring and exciting for youth.

Whether via an advertisement or through careful product placement, images of alcohol in the media have become ubiquitous. A recent study funded by the Office of National Drug Control Policy (ONDCP) examined top-rated television network series broadcast between October and December 1998.

The results: alcohol was consumed in 71 percent of all episodes, including 65 percent of the programs most popular with teenagers. About one-third of all the episodes were set in bars, nightclubs or restaurants where alcohol was consumed. Forty percent of the episodes made drinking look like a positive experience, while only 10 percent portrayed alcohol use negatively. Only one percent of the episodes portraying alcohol usage showed a refusal to use alcohol.

With happy hours, discounts on wine coolers and nickel-beer nights at bars near colleges, alcohol may be society's least expensive drug, but it is one of its most costly. Underage drinking costs the United States more than $58 billion every year—enough to buy every public school student a state-of-the-art computer.

Couple that with 1998 figures which calculate that alcohol-related traffic crashes cost this country $18,242,000,000 and you begin to see the devastating losses. But society pays a larger price than a monetary one. The death rate associated with youth alcohol use is staggering. Alcohol kills 6.5 times more youth than all other illicit drugs combined. The three leading causes of death for 15- to 24-year-olds are automobile crashes, homicides and suicides—alcohol is a leading factor in all three.

It would make sense, then, for the government to initiate and commit to a full-force effort to eradicate youth alcohol use. Surprisingly, when the federal government launched a five-year, $1 billion youth anti-drug media campaign, alcohol was excluded.

The Power of the Drug Alcohol

Alcohol itself—and the powerful nature of its effects on young bodies— is also a mighty force in America's No. 1 youth drug problem.

To put it simply, the effects of alcohol are seductive, potent and hazardous. Alcohol has absolutely no beneficial effects on teenagers, and its use needs to be taken seriously for what it is—perilous.

"Alcohol interacts with many different systems," explained Scott Swartzwelder, Ph.D., clinical professor at Duke University and coauthor of *Buzzed: The Straight Dope About the Most Used and Abused Drugs from Alcohol to Ecstasy.* "It causes sedative effects and relieves anxiety, among other things. In teens, there is less of a sedative effect and that is dangerous and misleading for teens."

"The brain systems that give drinkers positive feelings may adapt to the alcohol and come to need it," Dr. Swartzwelder continued. "After repeated use, the brain systems come to feel that something is missing when alcohol is denied, and this motivates people to drink even more. Eventually, people drink to prevent the negative effects they feel from not drinking."

The adolescent brain is particularly susceptible to the powerful effects of the drug alcohol. "We know that alcohol consumption can impact learning and memory in the adolescent brain," Dr. Swartzwelder said. "The dangers and long-term consequences of alcohol use among teens are not fully understood."

"Alcohol is the silent enemy," said Suzanne Smith, director of planning for operations at Phoenix House in Texas, the nation's leading substance abuse treatment, prevention and education organization. "Underage drinking remains a consistent problem. Society makes it accessible, and since it's legal for adults, the rules are confusing for adolescents. They don't really understand that alcohol is harmful to them."

In addition, alcohol is "the gateway drug" insofar as it's the precursor to teenagers trying many other types of substances. "Just about every kid who's being treated for drug abuse is mixing their drug of choice—be it marijuana or heroin or something else—with alcohol," said Smith.

According to Smith, "Most adolescents don't seek treatment on their own, and a parent, caretaker or more often than not the criminal justice system guides them to the help they need. Unfortunately, there are few long-term treatment programs available that provide teens with the structure they need to effect lasting changes in their behaviors, attitudes and values. As a result, only 10 percent of those who need help actually get it," so the problem can spiral out of control.

But treatment can work, and teenagers can be taught how to reclaim their lives by learning how bad alcohol really is for their bodies and for their future. "Treatment is really the second line of defense," Smith added. "Parents are unquestionably their children's first and most important teachers. They need to have heart-to-heart talks with their kids and give them accurate information about consequences of abusing alcohol and other substances."

Treatment is a win-win proposition: helping kids deal with their addiction and lead sober lives paves the way for them to become constructive, contributing citizens. And for every dollar society spends in treating addicted teens, it saves $12 on the criminal justice, health care and welfare systems.

First Steps for Alcohol-Free Youth

Greg Hamilton has been the chief of law enforcement of the Texas Alcohol Beverage Commission (TABC) for nearly seven years, and he said he's beginning to see a change nationwide.

"People in communities across the country are starting to get on board with this issue, but it takes time," he said.

"The TABC attacks the problem of underage drinking with a two-pronged approach: enforcement and education," he said. "We want to elicit voluntary compliance with the law by holding parents, kids, store owners and other adults responsible for giving or selling alcohol to minors. We take action against them and issue citations. We hold them accountable for their actions, and we educate them about the underage-drinking problem."

The TABC also educates law enforcement agents about the issue. "Law enforcement, like any other agency, is short staffed," Hamilton noted. "They used to tend to see underage drinking as a low priority, thinking that 'kids would be kids' and go through a drinking phase. But lately, police, store owners and parents are beginning to take the issue more seriously and doing something about it."

Still, more can be done. "Parents need to send a clear message that kids are not allowed to drink, and stop providing alcohol to their kids," he said. "High schools and colleges need to hold kids accountable for their actions when they buy or consume alcohol. And faith groups need to talk about the problem and educate the community."

Facing Reality

We can no longer point fingers at "bad kids" or negligent parents. Society as a whole bears the burden of the tragic consequences of underage drinking. MADD says that efforts to tackle the problem must involve parents—who, in their best efforts, can sometimes make uninformed and dangerous decisions. Retailers and the law enforcement community must strengthen their resolve to uphold the existing laws designed to protect young people. The media must be diligent in responsibly and accurately portraying the dangers of alcohol use by teens. Advertisers must cease targeting young people in marketing alcohol and alcohol-related products. Those who produce television shows and movies must take responsibility for the underage-drinking images they portray. Communities nationwide must provide treatment centers to help young people work their way back to alcohol-free lives. We must partner with youth.

Youth have emerged as a major force in the efforts to tackle underage drinking. All across the nation, young people are banding together to put an end to America's No. 1 youth drug problem. They not only are taking action—they are making a difference.

By linking arm-in-arm with these young people, we can eradicate the nation's most devastating youth drug problem—alcohol.

CRANKED UP

Jessica L. Sandham

Abuse of methamphetamine—also known as "ice," "crystal," and "crank"—is a serious problem for many teens, as Jessica L. Sandham writes in the following selection. According to the author, meth is appealing to teens who crave its powerful high and the seemingly unlimited energy that it provides. Furthermore, Sandham states, meth is an inexpensive and popular drug that is easy for teens to buy, make, and sell. The author notes that the ineffectiveness of traditional drug education programs and ignorance on the part of some parents and teachers have aggravated the problem. New approaches that involve schools and teachers in intervention and treatment for teen meth addicts are meeting with some success, she reports, but that success has been limited. Sandham is a staff writer for *Education Week*.

If it hadn't been for the help of her high school counselor, Charla Witcher believes, crank would have killed her.

Though she's been clean for more than a year, the 18-year-old senior at Natrona County High School still wakes up every morning with scars on her arms and cravings for the drug—physical remnants of a powerful addiction that turned this middle-class teenager into a dropout, a vandal, and a burglar before she finally broke the chokehold that methamphetamine had on her life.

She visits Jim Johnson's tiny office on the third floor of the high school once a week, sometimes more, in an effort to stay straight.

"I want to help people the way Jim helps people," says Witcher, who hopes to go to college to become a teacher after she graduates this year. "In a way, he saved my life."

While Witcher's story is dramatic, it is by no means unique in Casper, a commercial hub of 45,000 residents in the center of a rural state with three times as many cattle as people. Like their counterparts in many other towns in the West and Midwest, community leaders here have been working to conquer escalating methamphetamine use over the past several years. While meth, or "crank," as it is commonly known, is still mostly abused by adults in their 20s and 30s, law-

Reprinted from "Cranked Up," by Jessica L. Sandham, *Education Week*, May 24, 2000, by permission of *Education Week*.

enforcement and school officials say the potent stimulant has found its way into the hands of many teenagers—often with devastating results.

"This stuff is so strong and so debilitating that kids who use it go downhill so quickly," says Wayne Beatty, the safe-schools administrator for the 12,000-student Natrona County district. "They drop out of school and end up in the criminal-justice system."

With counselors trained in how to deal with substance-abuse issues in every high school and junior high, and education programs that tell teachers how to spot early signs of drug use, district officials here say they are working to get help as quickly as they can to the students who need it. Local instructors for the Drug Abuse Resistance Education, or DARE, program and other teachers also talk about meth during drug education classes. They hope students will steer clear of the drug once they learn about its consequences.

While marijuana and alcohol are still far more popular with young people here, school officials say methamphetamine use—even among a relatively low percentage of students—is simply too destructive to ignore.

"Meth gets a hold of kids, and by the time you find out, they're very harmfully involved," says Patricia Silva, a nurse at Natrona County High School. "It's a very rapid downward spiral."

Charla Witcher knows all about such downward spirals. She says she started experimenting with marijuana at age 13, then graduated to meth two years later when her father introduced her to the drug.

She watched him shoot up in front of her, she recalls, and wanted to experience it herself.

"It was a really neat high at first—you did it and it was just this explosive amount of energy," Witcher says. "My dad's philosophy was if I was going to do it, and I did it in front of him, it was OK."

Attempts to reach Witcher's father for comment were unsuccessful.

But the early highs soon plunged into crippling lows, and by the time she was 16, Witcher was doing meth nearly every day just to get out of bed in the morning. Without it, her body ached and even everyday tasks became difficult. She was working with her counselor, Johnson, at the time, but became concerned that teachers and fellow students knew too much about her drug use. She dropped out of school.

Though she is almost 6 feet tall, Witcher dropped to 120 pounds, and her skin turned gray.

She began stealing from family and friends to support her habit, and later burglarized a local antiques store, intending to hawk the wares in Denver so she could buy more meth. Arrested for the crime, she then broke her probation agreement and ran away from Casper with a boyfriend and another friend.

Witcher's mother, who is divorced from her father, said the time when her daughter was missing was perhaps the hardest of all.

"You don't sleep," says Elene Medicraft, who works as a computer clerk at the high school. "As a parent, you sit there and think, 'Is she alive or is she dead?' I really thought I was going to get a call in the spring, when the ranchers do their fence lines, and hear that they had found her body."

She got a call from her daughter instead. Witcher had been abandoned by her traveling partners across the state in Rock Springs and wanted to come home. When she arrived, she was arrested and sentenced to attend the Wyoming Girls' School, a correctional facility for juvenile offenders. She stayed drug-free during the nine months she was there, but slipped up after she was home for a month and exposed to her old life. Johnson and her mother and teachers held a meeting with Witcher to intervene, and she got the message. She says she has been clean ever since.

"Every day I wake up with the pain and the memories," says Witcher, who has served on several local panels in an effort to educate community members about the drug. "I try to make them understand what it does to people."

Wyoming law-enforcement officials say that the current wave of methamphetamine use first reared its head in this community and elsewhere in 1993, though it is hardly a new phenomenon. The drug once carried the street name of crystal meth, or "ice," and was also popular in the 1960s and 1970s. Crank is a powdery upper that can be injected, snorted, smoked, or even eaten—options that make the drug more socially acceptable to users who wish to steer clear of needles.

Part of meth's appeal to some young people is that the drug works by stimulating the nervous system like cocaine, making people at first feel euphoric, capable, and full of life. Users can initially stay up all night and still function and concentrate the next day, even perform better on tests than they did while not using it, said Dr. Berton J. Toews, a local psychiatrist who serves on the Natrona County district's safe- and drug-free schools advisory panel.

"It's an incredibly powerful drug," Toews says. "There's probably nothing in the world that feels better than your first use of coke or meth."

But unlike a cocaine high, which lasts for a couple of hours at most, a crank high often lasts for a full eight to 14 hours. In addition, the drug initially enhances sexual feelings and works as an appetite-suppressant—a side effect of the drug that makes it alluring for body-conscious young women who would do just about anything to lose weight.

Johnson remembers a girl who thinned down significantly in the early stages of a meth habit, and feared that stopping her use of the drug would bring the pounds back.

"She said, 'I do meth because guys like me now that I'm so skinny,'"

Johnson says. "Two weeks later, she was gone. She just dropped out."

Methamphetamine is also much cheaper to buy than cocaine and some other drugs. For just $60 a gram, "you can be up night and day," says Bryan Gimbel, an 18-year-old who attends the district's Rebound School, an alternative program for students who can't attend traditional high schools for disciplinary or personal reasons. "Last summer, I probably slept just three weeks out of the whole summer."

And though the drug is perhaps not as easy to come by as alcohol, students here say they don't have to look too long or far to find it.

Sabrina Schossow, an 18-year-old attending the Rebound School, says many students see meth as a natural next step when they want to get high more cheaply and quickly than they can with marijuana. "After pot, you do crank," says Schossow. "There's usually somebody who knows somebody who knows how to get it."

State officials say their efforts to beat back the onslaught of meth are made more challenging because the drug takes multiple routes into communities and into dealers' hands.

Much of the local meth supply is imported to the state from California and Mexico. But the drug can also be cooked up easily by local dealers, who can buy several hundred dollars' worth of such ingredients as over-the-counter cold or asthma medicine, drain cleaner, battery acid, and iodine to produce several thousand dollars' worth of meth. Recipes for the drug are widely available on the Internet. And while meth labs might be more readily detectable in densely populated areas—the cooking process emits a strong stench similar to that of cat urine—Wyoming's wide open spaces and blustery winds make it fertile ground for meth production.

"You can be a high school dropout at age 16 and cook up $500 worth of crank for $20 in materials and make a pretty good living," says Carol Eckstrom Hardy, the supervisor of New Horizons, a local residential drug-treatment center. "And here, you can drive up and down the interstate and cook it in the back of a van if you want to. It's been done."

Wyoming's law-enforcement agents have clamped down on meth dealers and producers over the past several years. They expect to break up at least 50 meth labs throughout the state this year, compared with only two such busts in 1997. In addition, state lawmakers recently approved a $5.5 million anti-meth initiative for the upcoming biennial budget cycle, most of which will go toward treatment and prevention education. Schools and other community organizations must play a role in decreasing the demand for the drug, state leaders say, if the state is ultimately to win its war on meth.

"If you don't cut the demand, you don't solve the problem," says Wyoming Gov. Jim Geringer. "Schools are among the first to know if something is wrong with kids. Parents are among the last to know."

To that end, the state division of law enforcement is now piloting a comprehensive, multiyear life-skills curriculum that addresses methamphetamine and other drugs. State officials say they hope the program will fill the gaps left by DARE programs, like the one in Natrona County, that serve students in only one grade. "You can't expect that a 16-week program will be enough to keep a kid off of drugs for life," says Thomas J. Pagel, the director of the state's criminal-investigation division. "It has to be a consistent message that builds from year to year."

Beatty of the Natrona County district acknowledges the limitations of the DARE program, in which local police officers talk to 6th graders about the dangers of drug use. But he says the school system's program is strengthened by the fact that drug education is also woven into life-skills education in other grades. When districts believe that all they need is DARE, he says, they're setting themselves up for failure.

Timothy McIntire, an officer with the Casper Police Department who teaches DARE classes at five elementary schools, says he often brings in popular 9th graders who don't use drugs or alcohol at parties to serve as role models for the 6th graders. He also discusses meth, using a display board to show students what the drug looks like and describing its toxic ingredients and crushing impact on users. Because meth overstimulates and thereby weakens the heart, users run the risk of suffering a heart attack or stroke long after they've stopped using the drug.

"It's out there, it's easy to get, and it's just so addictive," McIntire says. "We even have junior high school students using it. That's the really scary thing."

Thomas James, a 17-year-old junior at the Rebound School, sees the district's DARE program as a waste of time and money. Providing information about drugs to students interested in doing them, he says, is only going to pique their curiosity.

"The thing that DARE does is give kids a selection," he argues. "It's like a menu for drugs."

But at the Wyoming Girls' School, where 59 percent of the school's 90 students say they have used meth in the past, 17-year-old Tara says she never knew what exactly crank was when she was doing it—and that the information might have made a difference to her.

"I cannot believe I smoked that stuff and shot it into my veins," says Tara, whose 25-year-old then-boyfriend supplied her with the drug when she was 16.

Her classmate, 17-year-old Erica, agrees. School administrators requested that the girls' last names not be used.

"I never even heard about meth when I was young," says Erica, who started using the drug when she was 12. "I think if younger kids had information on it, it might get them to think."

Natrona County school officials say that teachers—who have regular contact with students but lack the emotional involvement that can skew parents' perceptions—are in an ideal position to recognize drug use in teenagers and intervene while it is still in the early stages.

The district is working to increase the possibility of such interventions by offering a five-evening course several times a year for teachers on how to recognize potential drug abuse by students. Teachers can sign up for the voluntary 3½-hour classes to fulfill professional-development requirements or gain college credit.

In one recent session, Beatty brought in a panel of students who were knowledgable about drug use in the community to talk about the scope of the problem among Casper's teenagers. The 54-year-old safe-schools administrator, whom many characterize as a powerful force behind the district's drive to combat substance abuse generally and methamphetamine use in particular, also leads a session specifically focusing on crank. He tells teachers to look for common side effects that meth users—sometimes known as "tweakers"—often share: rapid weight loss; unusual acne, welts, or skin blemishes; and erratic or cranky moods. He acknowledges that this last symptom can be tricky to distinguish from typical adolescent behavior.

Teachers who spot signs of drug use are encouraged to talk to school administrators about their suspicions.

"We need to make those connections so that everyone is helping and watching, and everyone is responsible," says Stan Olson, the district's superintendent.

Despite such efforts, the district has rarely cracked down on students for possessing meth, or being under its influence. Last school year, by contrast, the district took action against 114 students for having or using marijuana in school, and 69 students for using alcohol. Only one student was reported for meth, and there were just three meth-related reports the year before.

But district administrators say such numbers don't reflect what they hear anecdotally about meth use, and know about it from state statistics. Recent school surveys show that meth use among students in Wyoming is approximately three times the national average, says Pagel of the state division of criminal investigation.

"It's easy for a district to hide its head or turn away in the face of information like that," Pagel says. "You have to give the Natrona County school district a lot of credit. They've been right out in front in dealing with this."

School officials typically suspend students they suspect of any drug use or possession during school hours, and they give parents information about arranging for a drug test if a student wishes to contest the school's charges. Students facing drug charges for the first time would not be suspended for more than 10 days, and then would be given a chance to correct their behavior.

By referring suspected drug users to in-school counselors who meet with such students regularly and confidentially, district officials also say they are working to treat substance abuse as more of a health concern than a disciplinary matter.

The Natrona County district has a $320,000 annual contract with the Central Wyoming Counseling Center, a nonprofit organization, to provide 18 certified counselors to cover the district's 33 schools. The junior high schools and high schools have access to counselors on an almost full-time basis, while the elementary schools share the counselors' time. In an era when some districts are economizing by cutting counseling, Natrona County increased its budget for counseling services by 14 percent from fiscal 1998 to fiscal 1999. Beatty says the budget boost can be linked to the social ills students are increasingly dealing with at home that are "related to, but not exclusively tied to, meth use."

But while relationships like the one between Jim Johnson and Charla Witcher exemplify the good that can come from counseling programs, not every drug user will be reached that way. Johnson must get approval from the parents of students referred to him before he can sit down with them—a hurdle he says he can't always clear.

"The hardest thing I have to deal with is the indifference of parents and the denial kids have about their abuse," Johnson says. "There are kids here who are drug users who avoid me like the plague."

The district also gives students another therapeutic outlet for help: support groups. High school and junior high school teachers who have been trained to guide such sessions sit down with interested students in different groups one period a week, during school hours, to help them cope with such problems as depression and parents' divorces. The district pays substitutes to fill in for the teachers for that one period, in addition to covering the cost of the teachers' training.

The district's primary goal for the program is to connect students with adults and peers who care about them, says Silva, the school nurse, who coordinates the support-group program at Natrona County High, known as Student Assistance in Life, or SAIL.

Students who meet with Johnson for substance-abuse counseling later get together in the so-called recovery support group.

Though district leaders consider the 11-year-old SAIL program a success, they have learned not to expect cookie-cutter results.

Success in the substance-abuse small group might mean that a student didn't drop out this year, passed three out of six classes, or cut back on the amount of drugs he or she uses, Silva says. It is less likely to mean that a student has stopped using all drugs or alcohol—something she says is rare.

"Abstinence may not be everything," Silva suggests. "My yardstick for whether these groups are successful is if the kids keep coming. If the kids keep coming, they're getting something out of it."

But Tara and other former meth users at the girls' school say that even their local schools' best-intentioned efforts fell on deaf ears. If you're a teenager bent on numbing yourself with chemicals, they say, you're not likely to be interested in accepting help.

"I was approached by teachers several times," says Tara, whose physical reaction to the drug was so consuming that she sometimes chewed off pieces of her own tongue.

"I could have had all the help in the world," she says. "I just didn't choose to use it."

The Increase in Heroin Addiction Among Teenage Girls

Donna Leinwand

Heroin, an illegal drug that was popular in the late 1960s and early 1970s, is making a comeback among teens, especially girls. In the following article, Donna Leinwand discusses the reasons behind heroin's renewed popularity. Heroin is more potent and pure than ever before, Leinwand explains, enabling users to sniff or smoke the drug instead of inject it. This change has made heroin far more appealing to teenage girls, who tend to avoid drugs that must be injected. In addition, she notes, teenage girls are attracted to the look of "heroin chic" that has recently become a part of popular culture in the United States. Leinwand is a staff writer for *USA Today*.

Simona Troisi was a high school freshman on Long Island, at 14 already a user of marijuana and LSD, when she gave $40 to a friend to score some cocaine in New York City. The friend returned with a powder that gave Troisi a sickening high when she snorted it.

"I don't even know what it was," Troisi says. "I just kept doing it because I had it."

The strange powder was heroin, and within a few months, Troisi's recreational drug habit became a destructive lifestyle. She landed in a drug rehabilitation program after being charged with selling heroin to an undercover police officer. She had turned to dealing to help finance her appetite for tiny, $10 bags of the drug.

Now 20 and nine months into rehab, Troisi symbolizes how thousands of girls across the USA have fueled a dramatic resurgence of heroin use among teenagers, particularly in suburban and rural areas. Not since the late 1960s and early 1970s, when a typical dose was much less potent and almost always injected, has heroin been so hip among middle-class teens.

More Girls Are Using Heroin

Heroin's re-emergence comes at a time when girls—once far less likely than boys to drink, smoke marijuana or use harder drugs such as heroin—now appear to be keeping pace with them, says Mark Weber, spokesman for the federal Substance Abuse and Mental Health Services Administration.

Weber's agency, after finding that existing drug prevention programs helped reduce drug use only among boys, recently helped create an advertising campaign called "Girl Power" to deliver anti-drug messages specifically to girls.

A television commercial now airing features Olympic figure skating champion Tara Lipinski and Brandi Chastain, a member of the 1999 U.S. Women's World Cup soccer team, urging girls not to "blow it" by using drugs. The agency also has begun an unprecedented effort to collect statistics on girls' drug use.

The new surge in heroin use made national news with the overdose deaths of more than a dozen teenagers in Plano, Texas, and suburban Orlando, Florida, in 1996. Since then, hospital emergency rooms on Long Island, N.Y., and in the San Francisco Bay Area, the Philadelphia suburbs and several other middle-class areas have been hit by clusters of teens on heroin.

"The picture is frightening," says Mitchell Rosenthal, a psychiatrist and president of a chain of drug treatment centers who testified before the Senate Caucus on International Narcotics Control on May 9, 2000, about the emerging heroin problem in the suburbs. "We've got a lot of suburban kids at risk. I don't think the modern affluent parent thinks about heroin being a danger in Scarsdale or Beverly Hills."

One of four teenagers who testified is Kathryn Logan, 19, of San Juan Capistrano in southern California. At 9, Logan stole sips of wine from unfinished glasses. At 13, she rifled through medicine cabinets for prescription drugs she could chop up and sniff. She packed the powder into ballpoint pen casings so she could get high during class. At 15, she snorted heroin and cocaine and smoked crack.

"I felt more normal when I was on drugs," says Logan, who developed bulimia, had an abortion and tried to commit suicide. "I felt being sober was too boring."

To pay for her habit, she stole money from her parents and at one point pawned her grandmother's diamond ring for $25.

Even so, she kept up her grades, made the junior varsity tennis team and tried out for cheerleading. But she felt she didn't fit in at school, where she thought the people were "rich and stuck up." Her father, a contractor, and her mother, a flight attendant, didn't seem to notice her drug use.

"I was always making up excuses. I had everything under control, the whole world under control. It was hard, let me tell you," says Logan, who entered rehab in February 2000 to avoid going to jail on alcohol and marijuana possession charges. "My parents were clueless. I think they were in total denial that I was doing drugs until I told them about it."

Making Heroin Attractive to Girls

Heroin use remains relatively rare among teens overall. A study by the University of Michigan in 1999 estimated that about 2% of youths ages 12–17 had tried it. However, that was more than double the rate of seven years earlier. The same study indicated that 2.3% of eighth-graders in the USA, about 83,160 youths, had used heroin.

Analysts continue to examine the reasons behind the surge. There are the usual factors: teen angst, peer pressure, boredom, the attraction of something dangerous for teens with money to spend. But analysts say it's also clear that new, highly potent forms of heroin from drug cartels in Colombia and Mexico have been key to attracting new users—particularly girls.

For years, most heroin had to be injected directly into a user's bloodstream to be effective. Girls typically prefer to sniff or smoke their drugs rather than inject them, so heroin was out of vogue, experts say. But now, with more potent heroin available as a powder in small bags or gel capsules, users can get high without injecting. That has made it more palatable to girls.

"Young girls don't like injecting regularly. It leaves marks. With the increase in purity of heroin, it made it smokable," Sen. Joseph Biden, D-Del., says. As co-chairman of the Senate narcotics caucus, Biden issues regular reports on drug abuse.

"We are seeing a wider range of users," says H. Westley Clark, a psychiatrist and director of the federal Center for Substance Abuse Treatment in Washington, D.C. "We have been seeing younger people use. It has been fairly dramatic. These drugs are becoming equal opportunity drugs. There is no gender bias."

Lynn Ponton, a San Francisco–area psychiatrist, says that just a week ago a 17-year-old girl she is counseling tested positive for heroin in a routine drug screening.

"Traditional gender roles associated with risk-taking are not holding . . . for drug abuse," says Ponton, who wrote *The Romance of Risk*, a book about adolescent risk-taking. "Once (a drug is) available and hasn't been used for a long time, it's deemed cool by the teenagers. Heroin is still considered a super-cool drug, and it has high risk associated with it. It's probably the mystique of the drug."

Like the stimulant and hallucinogen Ecstasy, another favorite drug of the moment, heroin plays to girls' insecurities. Users lose their appetite, and so lose weight. The "heroin girl" look has been glamorized recently, from ashen, wafer-thin runway models to anthems by grunge bands.

All this has recast heroin in a more favorable light for this generation of youths. Troisi, who is 5 feet 5 and weighed 80 pounds when she entered drug treatment, says she never associated heroin with images of needle-toting junkies from the 1960s and '70s.

"Think of all the heroin-chic pictures that have been in the culture for a number of years," Rosenthal says. "Advertising campaigns show gaunt men and women. The stigma of heroin appears to have faded."

Producing and Marketing Heroin

Heroin, a narcotic derived from the opium poppy, was developed in the 1880s as a pain reliever and substitute for highly addictive morphine. Scientists soon found that heroin is even more addictive. It was made illegal in the United States in 1914. Heroin is produced mainly in Southeast Asia, Pakistan, Afghanistan, Mexico and Colombia.

For street sales, heroin is mixed, or "cut," with other ingredients, such as quinine or sugar. A hit of heroin produces a rush of euphoria followed by several hours of relaxation and wooziness.

Twenty years ago, a milligram dose with 3.6% pure heroin (and cut with 96.4% other ingredients) cost about $3.90, says Richard Fiano, director of operations for the Drug Enforcement Administration. Now, the average milligram is 41.6% pure and costs about $1. Some Colombian heroin the DEA seized recently was 98% pure, Fiano says.

Colombian drug lords used existing cocaine distribution networks to introduce the purer heroin to the USA, Fiano says. "They have a very, very good marketing strategy," he says. "They've come out with a new product line. They even have packaged it with brand names, just like buying a pack of cigarettes. They even gave out free samples."

The strategy appears to be working; heroin users are younger than ever. Surveys by the U.S. Substance Abuse and Mental Health Services Administration indicate the average age of first-time users plummeted from about 27.4 years in 1988 to 17.6 in 1997, the youngest average since 1969.

Emergency-room doctors reported in 1997 and 1998 that heroin is involved in four to six visits out of 100,000 by youths ages 12 to 17, up from one in 100,000 in 1990. For young adults 18 to 25, 41 emergency room visits in 100,000 involved heroin, up from 19 in 1991. Among women in general, the numbers have doubled in a decade.

Combating Heroin Abuse

Biden would like to direct more federal money to drug treatment for adolescents and law enforcement efforts in Colombia. Sen. Charles Grassley, R-Iowa, chairman of the Senate narcotics caucus, says that even if the USA directs more money toward Colombia, the focus should be on sending teens a clear anti-drug message, similar to the Reagan administration's "Just Say No" campaign.

Troisi says a steady stream of information about the risks of different drugs might have steered her away from heroin. She and her friends had no idea how seductive and addictive the drug could be, she says. She adds that she had no trouble finding heroin in her affluent hometown, Selden, N.Y.

"I'm not saying that heroin is the normal thing, but it is going more mainstream," she says. "When I first started, I was one of the first females, but I've seen more and more. I've seen them come into detox."

In Selden, about 45 miles from New York City, there isn't a whole lot for teens to do, and becoming a drug user wasn't too different from finding a spot in an after-school club, she says.

"It seemed like this underground society," says Troisi, who says she grew up in a stable home with three brothers, including one who was high school valedictorian. Her father is a high school teacher. "Boredom played a big part of it. A lot of my friends got involved in drugs real young. I kept away from it for a while, but I was real lonely. When I started using heroin, I just kept going back to it. I felt like I'd never feel comfortable with myself without it."

Like many girls who slide into addiction, Troisi wound up taking heroin the way she initially avoided: by injection. That way, Troisi, who sometimes spent more than $100 a day on drugs, needed less heroin to get high.

By the time she was 15, Troisi says, she loathed getting out of bed without a heroin jolt.

"I used to sleep with a bag of it in my bra so I would have it first thing, so I could get out of bed and brush my teeth," she says. Troisi, who after nine months of treatment now weighs a healthier 110 pounds, thinks she will get better. What she calls the "zombie" feeling has faded.

"One day, I woke up and I felt good," she says. "I eat now. And I go running, five miles a day sometimes. I feel like it's a new world. I still go through moods, but I know how to deal with those moods. I think I have a chance."

A NEW GENERATION OF DRUGS

Peter Vilbig

Well-known drugs such as marijuana, cocaine, and acid are not the only substances being abused by teens, as Peter Vilbig explains in the following selection. Teens looking for a new kind of high are increasingly experimenting with new drugs such as GHB and ecstasy, as well as mixing prescription drugs such as Xanax and Valium. Vilbig notes that these new drugs are often associated with "raves," or all-night dance parties, where ecstasy and other trendy drugs are considered an essential part of the experience. Teens are often unaware of the dangers of using these drugs, Vilbig cautions, believing that they are achieving a risk-free high. However, he writes, use of these drugs often has dangerous, if not fatal, consequences. Vilbig writes for *New York Times Upfront* magazine.

Samantha Reid left her room a mess that night. Clothes were tossed haphazardly over her bed in the quest for the perfect outfit. Magazines lay strewn among piles of stuffed animals. Telling her mom that she was going to a movie, the 15-year-old freshman at Carlson High School in suburban Detroit met up instead with two girlfriends. After a pit stop at a 7-11 for a Slurpee, they drifted to their real destination: an apartment in nearby Grosse Isle where four young men, two of them seniors, were waiting to hang out and watch videos.

The guys had their own plans to spice up the party. Unknown to Samantha and her friends, they had laced a few bottles of Mountain Dew with GHB, a feel-good chemical touted on the Internet as a safe, nonaddictive high that makes you feel drunk. What the Web sites don't say is that a slightly larger than normal dose can lead to coma and even death. Samantha drank hers down, and a few minutes later fell asleep on the couch. By the time the other partygoers brought her to an emergency room four hours later, she was already brain-dead. The next night she officially became one of the 65 GHB-related deaths since 1990.

Samantha's two friends were luckier. One recovered from a coma the next day. The other had turned down the spiked drink. As for the guys, three of them were found guilty of manslaughter in the spring of 2000 and were sentenced to 15 years in prison. The fourth will spend up to five years in jail on lesser charges.

"None of the girls ever knew the substance was put in their drinks," says Grosse Isle police detective John Szczepaniak, who investigated the case. "Samantha never knew what happened to her."

Ecstasy: A Trendy New Drug

GHB—otherwise known as Liquid X, Scoop, or Grievous Bodily Harm—is one of the substances that teens have recently begun to abuse with increasing frequency. Like teens of earlier generations, many teenagers today smoke pot, drop acid, or snort cocaine despite the known risks. But those drugs have been joined by others whose dangers are less well known: GHB, MDMA (also called ecstasy), and a potpourri of prescription pills. "What these kids don't know about these drugs is killing them," says Dr. Henry Kranzler, a psychiatrist at the University of Connecticut Health Center.

In recent years, illegal drug use by teens seemed to be coming under control. An annual survey conducted by the University of Michigan shows that teen drug use overall had soared by nearly 50 percent from 1991 to 1997, before dropping off in 1998 and holding steady in 1999. But a sudden 55 percent spike in teen ecstasy use in 1999, coupled with recent seizures of large caches of the drug, has raised fears that a new wave of teen drug abuse may be on the way.

Despite this sharp increase, only 8 percent of 12th-graders have tried ecstasy, the study found, making it far less popular than alcohol or marijuana. By the 12th grade, half of all students have tried marijuana. And alcohol remains by far the mind-altering substance of choice for most teenagers. The study found that 8 of 10 high school seniors have used alcohol, and more than 60 percent have been drunk. Alcohol also has the deadliest consequences of all drugs—for Americans ages 16 to 20, car crashes are the leading cause of death; in one recent year, 37 percent of those fatal accidents involved alcohol.

But ecstasy has become the trendiest of drugs, in large part because it is associated with dance music and raves. The speedy, slightly psychedelic high of ecstasy is widely seen as a no-risk buzz, without the potentially fatal side effects of heroin or GHB. While a few ecstasy-related deaths have been reported, they have come from heatstroke suffered by dancers at raves who didn't stop before severe dehydration set in. From the drug itself, most users report a sometimes severe, long-lasting hangover that leaves them feeling depressed.

But if the short-term effects don't seem horrendous, ecstasy could be a long-term nightmare. Scientists at Johns Hopkins University report that in studies on monkeys and humans the drug was found to cause brain damage, deforming a set of cells that may be important in mood regulation. Although several other studies show that ecstasy causes short-term memory loss and depression, some scientists say no clear evidence yet shows that the brain damage caused by the drug is permanent, or that it will lead to noticeable changes in brain function. More studies are needed, they say.

Despite ecstasy's reputation as a light drug, there's no doubt the little tablets, often stamped with well-known images ranging from the Nike swoosh to the Playboy bunny in an attempt to create brands, leave users heavily stoned. Menthol inhalers are sometimes used to enhance the drug's effects. "It's not unusual to walk into a club," says Miami Beach Police Chief Richard Barreto, "and see some individual zonked out in a trancelike state with one or two inhalers hanging out of his nose."

An Explosion of Ecstasy and GHB Use

Authorities fear a real explosion in ecstasy use has already begun. Seizures of the tablet have increased 450 percent from 1998 to 1999. "We are projecting seizures of up to 7 to 8 million pills [in 2000]," says Raymond Kelly, the commissioner of U.S. Customs. Many of those drugs will come from Israel and Russia, where organized crime has gone into the ecstasy exporting business.

The University of Michigan study doesn't cover the use of GHB, so there are no comparable statistics on its use, but several recent criminal cases show that its popularity is on the upswing, despite being one of the deadliest of the new drugs. GHB, or gamma hydroxybutyrate, was first developed for anesthesia during surgery, but in the last few years the tasteless, colorless liquid has become increasingly popular among teens for its capacity to produce feelings of euphoria, trippiness, and drunkenness. Since 1990, emergency rooms have reported 5,700 overdoses. The drug has also been called a "date-rape drug," after reports of 15 sexual assaults involving 30 victims drugged with GHB.

Users of GHB argue that the drug is natural because it occurs in the body. But a dose of the drug can be hundreds of times greater than the minute quantities found in the body. Also, with GHB, unlike with many other drugs, the difference between an overdose and a regular dose is extremely small. Because GHB is manufactured in kitchen shops, often with recipes downloaded from the Internet, it is usually impossible to know the quality and strength of each batch. The ingredients can include cleaning fluid and Red Devil lye, so production errors can create a fierce acid that burns the throat. After Samantha Reid's death, a new federal law signed in the winter of 1999 makes possession of GHB a crime punishable by up to 20 years in prison.

Mixing Prescription Drugs

Another trend involves the increased use of "cocktails" of prescription drugs, which are taken in widely varying combinations. According to interviews with experts and dozens of students around the country, highs from mixing prescription drugs are gaining more and more adherents, possibly because the drugs are cheaper and easier to get than street drugs.

The dangers of drug cocktails became apparent on the first day of spring break of 2000 at Trinity College, a small private school on a hilltop in Hartford, Connecticut. By 7:30 that morning, police had picked up William B. Bachman, a Trinity senior, after he had run his car into a fire hydrant. They took him to a nearby emergency room to be treated for possible drug ingestion. Within hours, one of Bachman's roommates, Joshua B. Eaves, arrived at the emergency room with what looked like a drug-induced illness. At 12:24 P.M., a third roommate, Josh Doroff, an intelligent, well-liked, and athletic freshman, was carried unconscious into the emergency room by three friends. He was pronounced dead a few minutes later. Police found a fourth roommate, Clement Kaupp III, unconscious at the students' apartment. Kaupp spent three days critically close to death before recovering.

Doroff's death stunned the campus community. An autopsy showed he had taken a cocktail of the anti-anxiety medications Xanax and Valium, sleeping pills, and other drugs. But many students say they are far from shocked to hear of heavy abuse of prescription drugs on campus. If it gives a buzz, they say, some students are willing to try anything.

"Even if it feels bad," says Peter LaBier, an art major at Vassar College in Poughkeepsie, New York, "it's just something that feels different. There's just this urge with kids my age to derange your senses."

The 1999 University of Michigan study found that one-fifth of college students interviewed had taken Ritalin, a drug for children who are hyperactive or have problems concentrating. But it also produces a speedy high that students favor for studying. Many also admitted using Dexedrine, another upper.

Feeling Invulnerable

The mix-and-match approach to drug use has attracted students who want to experiment with a different kind of high. "Once you get bored with drug X, you can try something new," says Mike Ferraro, a senior English major at Rutgers University in New Brunswick, New Jersey.

But miscalculations occur. Youthful feelings of power and control are at odds with the power of the drugs. "Kids feel a certain invulnerability, and they take risks," says Linda Campanella, Trinity's senior vice president.

Case in point: the high school seniors who gave Samantha Reid GHB never imagined she would die from it. Now her mother spends her evenings working on anti-GHB campaigns. "I'm trying as hard as I can to make some purpose out of my daughter's death," she says. "She can't die without a purpose, or I'd go out of my mind."

TEENAGERS AND COMPULSIVE GAMBLING

Bella English

Compulsive gambling is not a problem that is generally associated with teenagers, but as Bella English explains in the following selection, teens can be just as susceptible to the lures of gambling as adults. In recent years, she relates, gambling has become more accessible to teens than ever before. The flashy lights and sounds of the casino and the lure of hitting it big betting on sporting events, the author writes, have led to greater numbers of teens becoming addicted to gambling. English notes that teens who become addicted to gambling often have problems with other types of addiction, such as substance abuse. Overcoming an addiction to gambling is a life-long process that is just as difficult as overcoming addiction to drugs and alcohol, she concludes. English is a staff reporter with the *Boston Globe*.

Christopher adored gambling. The video poker, the slots, the dogs, his sports teams—each was as enticing as the next. He knew his way around the track blindfolded and would tear through the handicapping guides as if they were dime mysteries. He had his favorite set of poker machines at his casino of choice, Lincoln Park in Lincoln, Rhode Island.

He had his own bookie, too, who had noticed him one night playing the slots at Lincoln Park and asked if he wanted to make "some real money." His first sports bet with the bookie was like that first hit of heroin. Christopher was hooked. "Say you bet $1,000, and you lose it," he says. "You put $2,000 on the next game."

Like most gamblers—except maybe James Bond—Christopher lost a lot more than he won. Even after he dropped between $30,000 and $40,000 in just six months, he somehow found the money to feed his habit. To cover his debts, he indulged in what he calls "creative financing," including writing bad checks. He borrowed $400 from a friend and didn't pay it back. He filched relatives' ATM and credit cards. He stole from his sister. But no matter how much money he got his hands on, it was never enough.

Reprinted from "Old Game, New Players: For as Long as There Has Been Gambling, There Have Been Problem Gamblers. But They're Getting Younger All the Time," by Bella English, *Boston Globe*, February 21, 1999. Copyright © 1999 Boston Globe Newspaper. Used with permission of the *Boston Globe*, via the Copyright Clearance Center, Inc.

One night in May 1998, already deeply in debt, he went to the casino and blew another $500. In despair, he drove to a bridge and smoked a pack of cigarettes while pondering a plunge. Finally, a police officer moved him along. Christopher drove away in tears. Burdened by his addiction, he felt world-weary.

He was barely 18 years old. Gambling has been with mankind since ancient times. As Howard Shaffer, a psychology professor at Harvard University, likes to point out, Roman guards cast lots over Christ's robes during the Crucifixion. But what is new and troubling is the number of young people like Christopher who have become hard-core gamblers. A recent analysis by Shaffer shows that the rate of problem gambling among youths nationwide is more than double that of adults. Of the teenagers who gamble, nearly 10 percent will have a serious problem with it, compared with about 4 percent of adults.

In Massachusetts—with its popular lotteries and tracks and with casinos in nearby states—5 percent of the adult population, or about 250,000 people, have a gambling problem, although only about 2 percent are defined as "compulsive gamblers." Men are more likely to have trouble than women, but with the advent of readily accessible games like the lottery and Powerball, the gender gap is closing. Among the state's adolescents, 12 to 15 percent suffer from problem gambling, according to the Massachusetts Council on Compulsive Gambling.

Getting Hooked

For Christopher, it began innocently enough. He and some college buddies were sitting around the dorm drinking beer in the fall of 1997, his freshman year, and someone suggested a drive to the Newport Jai Alai and Casino in Rhode Island. The colorful flashes of the video games and the carnival noises of the slots were like the Pied Piper, beckoning him deeper and deeper into the gambling culture. Worst of all, Christopher got lucky. The hundred bucks he pocketed that night was chump change compared with the thousands he would later lose. His habit was financed in part by a campus job that paid nearly $10 an hour, a job he would eventually lose because of his habit. Gambling would come before everything else, including work.

During Christmas vacation that year, he headed to Lincoln Park Casino every day. The casino wasn't far from his home in a suburb south of Boston, and he loved betting the dogs over simulcast and playing video poker. It was easy money, better than flipping burgers at McDonald's, like other teens. One night, he won $700. The scene was way cool: the dim lighting, the older crowd, the clinking of mixed drinks, all of it wrapped in a blue veil of smoke.

In March 1998, Christopher stopped attending classes, though he continued to live in his dormitory. In April, his parents, who had no idea he wasn't in school, received their bank statements and confronted Christopher about large withdrawals. There was a big scene, with the mother crying, the father and son yelling. An ultimatum was delivered: Christopher could either attend Gamblers Anonymous meetings or be cut off from the family. "I didn't feel like being homeless," Christopher says. So he agreed to go to a meeting. Still, he continued to deny he had a problem. "Lots of college kids gamble," Christopher says. "If they don't go to the casino, they play poker or blackjack all night long. The difference is, not a lot of them have money. When I had $500 in my wallet, I felt like a big man on campus. I'd take a new kid to the casino, he'd win 20 bucks and be all jazzed and want to go again." What Christopher didn't know was that he had a disease he'd never heard of: pathological gambling. The American Psychiatric Association defines it as a mental disorder with symptoms that include a loss of control over gambling, a progression in frequency of wagering and the amount wagered, a preoccupation with betting, and a continuation of the gambling despite adverse consequences.

Compulsive Gambling

Unlike Christopher, most people can gamble without losing control. Even basketball superstar Michael Jordan, whose penchant for betting is well known, can't necessarily be labeled a problem gambler. "If Michael Jordan spends $50,000 on a golf game," says Shaffer, "he can afford that. He makes that money during a catnap, and you can't assume he's got a problem. But if you've got a kid who's spending $200 regularly and can't afford it, that's a problem. It's the consequences that define the problem."

And so it goes with compulsive gamblers like Christopher: They play, they lose, they play some more in an attempt to stay even. They can never get ahead. Much as an alcoholic will awake with a hangover and have a drink to steady his hands, a compulsive gambler will lose and play again and again and again. And much as an alcoholic will build up a tolerance to the bottle, a gambler builds up a tolerance to the loss. Gambling, like alcoholism, is a progressive disease: It's always just one more roll of the dice, spin of the wheel, or bet at the window.

Easy Access to Gambling

Shaffer and other experts believe the prevalence of legalized gambling in society is the reason kids are getting hooked. Pass any grocery store or gas station, and you will see lottery and scratch tickets on sale; in 1997, the Massachusetts Lottery sold more than $3.2 billion in games of chance, some of it to underage youths. Television brings you the lucky numbers. It's not unusual for parents and grandparents to buy even the youngest children scratch tickets for their birthdays or Christmas. Many churches sponsor weekly bingo nights. Most large newspapers publish point spreads in their sports sections.

Then there are the tracks, open to those 18 and older in Massachusetts, and the casinos in neighboring Rhode Island and Connecticut. And, according to Christopher and other young people, many high schools have their own resident bookie, a classmate with whom students place sports bets. The Internet also offers scores of gambling sites, where all you need is access to a computer and a credit card. Ready cash for the casinos and the track is more accessible these days, too, with an ATM seemingly on every corner.

"Kids today have grown up in this culture," says Kathleen Scanlan, director of the Massachusetts Council on Compulsive Gambling, a state agency that offers information and referral services to problem gamblers. "A lot of them are in a lot of trouble." Shaffer is even more blunt: "For some kids, gambling is the crack of the '90s."

It wasn't always this way. "When I was growing up," Shaffer says, "the nightly news led with the weather report. Now they lead with the winning lottery numbers." By the time teenagers are in their senior year of high school, he says, nationally, 90 percent have gambled. "Young kids gamble over pogs," colorful cardboard disks, with the victor taking the spoils, he says. "You can see the seeds being sown there."

Those seeds may take root in high school and spread in college: Addiction experts in Massachusetts are regularly called onto campuses to consult on gambling issues. In July 1997, the Middlesex district attorney's office ended a nine-month investigation into organized sports gambling at Boston and Bentley colleges by announcing the indictments of six men, some of them students, on 63 charges of illegal bookmaking. Earlier, the office had uncovered student-run bookie operations at both schools. Sports gambling is particularly popular with youths, because bets can be placed with no money up front.

Gambling Addiction Is a Disease

But gambling—both by youths and adults—is often swept under the rug, because it is the "invisible addiction." Even those closest to the gambler usually don't know the extent of the problem. "There aren't the physical signs you see with alcohol or drug abuse: the staggering, the stumbling, the slurring of words," Scanlan says. Nor is there the stigma; instead, there is what she calls the "acceptability and accessibility of it." Christopher's parents were shocked when they found out about their son's problem. "We're not gamblers, we're not drinkers, we're not smokers," says Christopher's father, Joseph. "We didn't even know about gambling, quite frankly."

Joseph went to the Gamblers Anonymous meetings with Christopher, to find out what, exactly, his eldest son was up against. Now he is a man with a mission. "It's become almost a ministry for me," says Joseph, who works in the computer industry and describes his large, close-knit family as "middle-class, vanilla-type people."

"For me and my wife," he says, "gambling is like cancer. It's a disease as deadly as cancer. It's one that can be dealt with through therapy and that one can learn to live with. We love our son. We don't want him to die. Every day that he is alive, there's a chance he will get better." Joseph is a big fan of Gamblers Anonymous. "You wouldn't think it," he says, "but from a father's perspective, there's a dozen great role models in that room."

Still, he has no illusions about the enemy his son is up against. In spring 1998, when Christopher was at his lowest point, he asked his father to bail him out. Joseph agreed to pay the $900 Christopher owed the bookie he'd met at Lincoln Park. If the money wasn't paid, Christopher told his father, he'd be beaten up or killed. Joseph accompanied his son to the appointed place—a convenience store in the town where Christopher attends college—to make sure the money actually got to the bookie. While the father waited in the car, the son went behind the building to pay off his bookie. When he returned to the car, Christopher thanked his dad. "He said, 'Boy, am I glad it's over. I'll never do it again.'"

But the money never reached the bookie. Several days later, Joseph learned that Christopher had pocketed the $900 and gambled it away almost immediately. The memory is still painful. "What was hard," Joseph says, "was that he could look us in the face and lie with such great conviction."

After learning his lesson the hard way, Joseph stopped bailing Christopher out. The men in Gamblers Anonymous reinforced that decision, saying he would just be enabling his son. "Like giving him a loaded gun" is the way one put it.

Why Do Teens Gamble?

Should parents help pay their teenagers' gambling debts? The question comes up all the time on the hot line run by the Council on Compulsive Gambling. "It's a very difficult decision," says JoAnn Cailler, the council's program director. "Sometimes, it means having to take a second mortgage on the home. Parents worry that they may be helping their child to gamble. But they may also worry about their child's safety. It's a real difficult place for a parent to be." No one really knows why some people are more vulnerable than others to compulsive gambling; why one teenager can bet occasionally on his favorite team while someone like Christopher bets hundreds of dollars a week. Shaffer, who is the director of the division on addictions at Harvard Medical School, says new evidence indicates that compulsive gambling may have genetic origins. "There is evidence of a biogenetic vulnerability," he says. "It does tend to run in the family, but then again, most families tend to grow up in the same house." A recent study also shows a link between gambling and other high-risk behavior among teenagers. Dr. Elizabeth Goodman of Children's Hospital in Boston surveyed 17,000 teenagers from Vermont. Fifty-three percent said they had gambled; 7 percent reported having a gambling problem. A closer look showed that those with a gambling problem also reported problems with alcohol and drugs. "Youths who had problems due to gambling were more likely to have used cocaine more than three times in the past month," says Goodman, whose study was published in the summer of 1998 in the *Journal of the American Academy of Pediatrics*.

Christopher fits that profile. He has had problems with binge drinking, has smoked marijuana since he was 12 years old, and has experimented with harder drugs.

"Pathological gamblers often are seeking a high through gambling," says Goodman. "The process of gambling is having some sort of physiological effect on the body. We don't know exactly what that effect is."

But gamblers do. It's mind-altering, they say, like cocaine; better than the best sex they ever had. Many gamblers will tell you that they literally shake, like an alcoholic, when placing a bet. Listen to Christopher: "For me, it's the high, the adrenaline, the thrill, the risk. There's nothing like it in the world. Nothing else matters when you're gambling."

Recovery from Gambling Takes a Lifetime

Those gamblers who are substance abusers swear that the bottle is easier to beat than the bet. Sam, 52, attends both Alcoholics Anonymous and Gamblers Anonymous meetings. "Gambling is a much more difficult addiction," he says. In his high school yearbook, Sam was named the "first man to take a gamble." That was 35 years ago; his youthful habit became an addiction that he still struggles with today.

"I thought it was really cool at the time," he says of his youthful gambling. "I've lost thousands and thousands and thousands of dollars. If kids get hooked, it will be a lifetime recovery process. It goes right to their heads. They think it's easy money, but there can be lifetime consequences."

Youths, who tend to be more risk-oriented than adults, also have an illusion of control over their gambling. "There's a sense that they have a special skill," says Howard Shaffer, "when there is no skill at all in gambling. That's why it is called gambling." Christopher attended his first Gamblers Anonymous meeting in May 1998. Every night, there is a Gamblers Anonymous meeting somewhere in the Boston area. Modeled after Alcoholics Anonymous, Gamblers Anonymous follows a similar 12-step program, starting with the acknowledgment that the gambler is powerless over gambling, that life has become unmanageable.

One may imagine that gamblers are all seedy-looking guys in polyester pants, with protruding bellies, beard stubble, and bleary eyes. A Gamblers Anonymous meeting will quickly dispel that myth. Many of the people who attend are middle-class; they hold jobs and pay taxes. Others have lost their jobs because of gambling and are attempting to dig their way out of a hole. Most of them are in their 40s, 50s, or 60s, but many describe a problem that started decades earlier.

You won't see many young faces at these meetings. The few who attend swear it has helped, but getting teenagers to go is difficult. They deny they have a problem, or their parents bail them out. Then there are more practical concerns: how to get to the meetings, for instance. Recently, two teenagers arrived at a meeting at Curry College in Milton, Massachusetts, by bus. They weren't yet old enough to drive, and their parents had no idea they were in trouble. Christopher is a rarity: His father attends the meetings with him.

Preventing and Treating Teen Gambling

Whether a gambler is young or old, there isn't much help available for the addiction. Nationally, there are 13,000 programs for substance abusers but fewer than 100 for people with gambling problems. Massachusetts spends a total of $1.1 million each year on problem gambling, of which $270,000 goes toward treatment programs, or a little more than a dollar per gambler. (Ironically, those funds come from unclaimed lottery receipts.) That money is divided among 17 treatment centers, most of them operating out of substance-abuse sites.

The oldest program is the Mount Auburn Hospital Center for Problem Gambling, which was established in 1989. The Cambridge center evaluates gamblers and offers individual psychotherapy as well as group and couples therapy. It also consults to Boston-area colleges.

"We're really interested in helping people understand what makes them do what they do," says Dr. Lance Dodes, a psychiatrist who serves as the clinic's director. He is hopeful about teenage gamblers, he says, for the same reason why he is hopeful about teenagers in general: They often grow out of their troubles. "Just as there are a lot of people who overdrink in college but don't go on to become alcoholics," Dodes says, "there are a lot of young people who gamble but don't go on to become compulsive gamblers. The problem is, compulsive gamblers often start early."

Like Gamblers Anonymous meetings, such centers do not see many young gamblers. "There's not a lot at stake at this point in their lives," explains Marilyn Feinberg, a therapist at the Mount Auburn center. "Compulsive gamblers who have families and have gotten into a lot of trouble, they usually have some hope of reconciliation with their wives, and that can be very helpful in getting them into your office and into treatment."

Prevention would naturally be the best "cure." But while teenagers are bombarded with information about the dangers of drinking, drugs, and sex, gambling gets little attention. When it can find a volunteer and a receptive school, the Council on Compulsive Gambling will send a recovering gambler to high schools to speak to students.

There are broader moves afoot to control the pervasiveness of gambling in society. Consumer-rights guru Ralph Nader has launched a campaign to make Las Vegas, which has invested heavily in child-oriented arcades and shows, less family-friendly. Howard Shaffer has been consulting with the gaming industry to help casinos develop guidelines on responsible gambling, which means no underage gamblers. In June 1999, President Bill Clinton's commission on compulsive gambling is expected to release a national report on the extent of gambling, including a section on youths, with recommendations for dealing with the problem.

Shaffer, who counsels compulsive gamblers, says cognitive therapy seems to work the best; that is, changing the way gamblers think about their behavior. More practically, it involves lifestyle changes, such as taking a different route home to avoid the track.

Together, Shaffer and his patients come up with a plan. Reestablishing meaning in their lives, whether it be from religion or relationships, works for some people. Others recover cold turkey, on their own. But for people who can't quit gambling that way, drugs such as those used for obsessive-compulsive disorder are being tested. "They're trying antidepressants and anti-anxiety agents," says Shaffer. "It's almost a shotgun approach to see which one works." Christopher's journey has been one step forward, two back; two steps forward, one back. He and his parents know the road to recovery is pocked with potholes.

Admitting to Addiction

At his first Gamblers Anonymous meeting, in a basement room of Southwood Community Hospital in Norfolk, Massachusetts, Christopher listened to the tales of men losing their wives, their homes, their kids, their sanity, their freedom. He still didn't get it. "I thought I was invincible. They're all old guys," he recalls.

Two days after that meeting, Christopher went out and gambled for three days running, losing $500. Shaken, he went to a second meeting, stood up, and announced, "I'm Christopher G., and I'm a compulsive gambler." It was the first time he'd admitted it, and it felt good.

But even after his admission, the grip of gambling proved too powerful. Christopher left that meeting and drove straight to Lincoln Park. In his pocket was $500, money he'd stolen from his sister and borrowed from friends. Within an hour, it was gone. Furious at himself, Christopher peeled out of the casino parking lot and drove to a bridge, where he parked his car and smoked cigarette after cigarette, flicking them into the water below. "I thought a jump might hurt for a second," he says now, "but then the pain will be over."

Christopher probably would not have jumped—"I'm a major chicken," he says. At any rate, the police car pulled up and the officer told him to move on. He drove home, remembering one of the tenets of Gamblers Anonymous: Write down your feelings and the damage your gambling has caused. In his room, Christopher scribbled non-stop. It all came out: the stealing, the lying, the cheating, the pain, the suicidal thoughts. Then, he woke his father and handed him the statement. Both were in tears.

That night, May 21, 1998, father and son once again attended a Norfolk meeting together. The summer unfolded nicely for Christopher. Accompanied by his father, he attended meetings faithfully. The older men were touched by Christopher; in him, they saw themselves 20, 30, or 40 years earlier. Christopher also enrolled in summer courses at his college to make up the credits lost to gambling in the spring.

In September, his parents accompanied him to a Gamblers Anonymous potluck. Christopher, who brought the potato salad and cole slaw, was the youngest one there by decades. "I feel like I'm one of them," he says. "I never lost a wife, a house, or kids to gambling. But I'm a compulsive gambler, and they're compulsive gamblers. I stole, they stole."

Besides absorbing horror stories from the men, he was picking up coping strategies: how to avoid a bet, how to use a buddy list. How, just as an alcoholic can't have even a sip, he couldn't bet even a quarter.

At a mid-September meeting, Christopher gave the group a sunny progress report. "On Friday night, there was a big back-to-school party. After, I went to a store and bought a scratch ticket, but I didn't scratch it; I gave it to my best friend. I took an algebra test, got into honors, and had a terrific job interview. Things are looking up." The men applauded.

The Rocky Road to Recovery

At that point, Christopher was 140 days clean. "I told the bookie I moved. I never carry more than $20 in my pocket. I'm the luckiest man on earth to get out of the hell I created for myself," he announced. Six weeks later, Christopher is sitting in a folding chair in the basement room of Southwood Community Hospital. His father sits next to him, studying the text intently while the young man fidgets in his seat like a bored child at church.

Tonight, Christopher will not stand up and share his story. There are too many people; he'd be embarrassed. Besides, the news isn't good. If he did stand up, here's what he says he would say: "Life sucks. I've been gambling again and doing drugs. Right now, I don't feel like coming here on Thursday nights. I'm listening, but I'm not absorbing it."

Christopher's road to recovery, which seemed so promising in early September, collapsed shortly after his college classes resumed. During his second week of school, he returned to Lincoln Park and blew $500 on the dogs and video poker. He began popping Ecstasy, a popular amphetamine on college campuses, and now feels he is saddled with two addictions. "I've been gambling to see if I can win money to pay off the drug dealer," he says. At the moment, he figures he owes $3,000 in gambling and drug debts, money his parents will no longer pay. Christopher has begun therapy and has started attending weekly Narcotics Anonymous meetings, too.

"It's a war," his father says. "And we're not about to give up. Do I have the answer today? No. Will we get through this? Yes."

Still, it is, as Gamblers Anonymous has told them, a war to be fought one day at a time. At this particular meeting, it has been 12 days since Christopher last gambled. Still, the urge is there. "The fall is really hard because of all the sports teams," Christopher says. "And Super Bowl Sunday will be terrible."

But in December 1998, Christopher's parents pull him out of school, because he is failing all of his classes. Christopher is now planning on joining the military to "get away from the drug and gambling culture and to grow up," his father says.

Christopher's advice to other kids in trouble with gambling? "Get help. Talk to people. Don't give up. Even if you slip and mess up again, you can still pull yourself out." He pops his knuckles and jiggles his leg nervously as he speaks. His handsome face is a mask of misery.

"I'm only 18," he says. "I don't want to end up at 58 losing my wife, my home, and my job. I'm 18, and I'm scared."

CHAPTER 2

WHAT ARE THE CAUSES OF TEEN ADDICTION?

TEEN ADDICTION IS A DISEASE

Nikki Babbit

In the following excerpt from her book *Adolescent Drug and Alcohol Abuse*, Nikki Babbit explains that most experts consider addiction to be a disease involving biological, psychological, and social factors. Although this disease is not yet fully understood, she writes, it is clear that some individuals are far more vulnerable than others. Teens who are at high risk may move quickly from experimenting with alcohol and drugs to full-blown addiction, Babbit maintains. Therefore, she cautions, it is crucial for parents to recognize the signs of substance abuse and to obtain help for addicted teens at an early stage of the illness. Babbit is a psychologist and adolescent and family therapist in Ohio who has been working with addicted teens and their families since 1965.

As children grow, parents watch them deal with such problems as rejection on the playground, not getting a star on a spelling test (despite practicing from their mother's dictation the night before), not being chosen for a sports team, or hearing about someone they know being killed in a traffic accident. Parents weather these disappointments with their children and try to offer their support. As children grow up, they may have to cope with other disturbing events, such as breaking up with a girlfriend or boyfriend; having to deal with death or divorce; having a parent lose their job; the family farm being sold to developers; having to adjust to a new school, a new neighborhood, or even a move across the country.

Parents know that events like these have an impact on children and adolescents. It is easy to think that "acting out" behaviors are a result of these events. Parents can feel sorry for young people who have gone through these struggles, and these feelings can help to justify their misbehavior, no matter how destructive. Parents may use such excuses for months or even years after the original event. . . .

Misconceptions About the Causes of Addiction

When adolescents start hanging around people their parents don't approve of or start doing things that result in legal trouble, it is easy to attribute these behaviors to normal adolescent rebellion. It is also easy to blame problems on new friends, peer pressure, or the wrong choices. Even when parents question the role that drugs might play, it is easy to dismiss it, particularly when the child denies there is a problem. One father relates his story:

> Our son was well on his way in his addiction, but when we questioned him about drugs maybe being a problem he was pretty angry. He said something like, "Do you really think I'd be that stupid?" We wanted to believe that his behavior was related to all the moves we had, and we had really taught him well about the dangers of drugs, so we believed him.

This father's story illustrates another misconception: if you teach your children well, they will not have problems with drugs. Parents and school personnel can overlook drug or alcohol abuse when they have a strong anti-drug education program in their home or school. The assumption is that this education will prevent abuse. That sounds logical, but it doesn't always work for all kids.

The mother of an alcoholic teen explains how she tried to educate her children about alcoholism:

> Both of my own parents had a lot of problems with alcoholism. They were even out of control when we had family visits with them. We talked about it at home with the idea that our kids would never choose this kind of life for themselves. We were sure that our kids got the point. I mean, how could they miss it?

A recovering alcoholic mother describes a similar misconception that results in blinders about drug and alcohol abuse:

> When my two daughters were growing up, I was in recovery. I even took them to AA meetings with me. I really beat myself up when I didn't see that they had the same symptoms that were part of my own alcoholism. I blamed these behaviors on other things. Since my girls saw how much happier I was without drinking, I thought that they would feel the same way. They certainly wouldn't choose the life of an alcoholic.

All of these misconceptions about the causes of alcoholism and addiction assume that potential addicts or alcoholics are capable of making decisions to control their substance use, and that they know the right thing to do. A teen addict/alcoholic who is now attending Alcoholics Anonymous (AA) meetings in order to remain sober and drug-free describes his blinders:

> I knew that my grandparents lost most of their lives because of alcoholism. I also lived in a loving home where my parents didn't have alcohol in the house, and we talked about the

dangers of addiction. So I thought that I would never be an addict. And I would make sure that if I drank, it would never get out of control. No way! I was too smart to let that happen.

Many writers, such as Claudia Black in her book, *It Will Never Happen to Me,* have explored the myth that knowledge allows a person to escape addiction. Black is an assessment professional who has diagnosed hundreds of adult and adolescent addicts. She explains:

> Knowledge can lead to a false sense of security where addiction is concerned. Family members of addicts are sure that it will never happen to them because they want to avoid inflicting the same pain on others. Parents think that because their child has been raised under the right circumstances, they will escape. The fact of the matter is, it can happen to anyone. Even when we think that it should happen to someone who had parents who were drunk around the kids or who lived with addicts next door, they escape. The disease is unpredictable. It provides equal opportunity to everyone.

Use, Abuse, and Dependency

Anyone, therefore, can become an alcoholic and addict, but many will also escape. As Vernon Johnson, DD, a world-recognized authority on alcoholism and addiction who died in 1999, explains:

> It's clear that all sorts of people become drug and alcohol dependent, some for no apparent reason. On the other hand, it seems that some people can't become dependent no matter how hard they try!
>
> We do know that drug and alcohol dependence isn't caused by a lack of will power, weakness of character, or some flaw in a person's moral structure. And it's not a form of mental illness. Nor is it the result of external influences—an unhappy marriage, trouble on the job, peer pressure.

Johnson reminds us that there is no absolute reason that explains the cause of addiction. There is a simple truth: no matter what parents have done, they did not cause their adolescent's drug abuse or addiction. . . .

How do abuse and dependency happen? The biopsychosocial disease model defines the disease of addiction as primary, progressive, chronic, and ultimately fatal if not arrested. The disease is characterized by the ongoing use of drugs or alcohol despite harmful consequences. It is also described as a no-fault illness, like diabetes, because alcoholics and addicts do not *choose* to be dependent. According to this model, treatment needs to address the biological, psychological, and social aspects of the disease.

This disease model is widely accepted by both physicians and professional groups all over the United States and Canada, and the model is emulated in many other areas of the world. . . .

The biopsychosocial disease model is used as the model for treatment by the American Medical Association, the American Psychiatric Association, the American Hospital Association, the American Public Health Association, the American Psychological Association, the National Association of Social Workers, the World Health Organization, and the American College of Physicians. It is also used as a model for treatment by the Joint Commission on Accreditation for Healthcare Organizations (JCAHO), by insurance plans in the United States that will help parents pay for their children's treatment, and by many provinces in Canada. In both the United States and Canada, certain aspects of the model may be emphasized more than others in treatment, and spiritual degeneration may also be addressed. . . .

The biological nature of addiction in particular is also an active area of research in hopes that some day there will be an effective way for addicts and alcoholics to use medication as one of the tools for recovery. Enoch Gordis, MD, director of the National Institute on Alcohol Abuse and Alcoholism, who presented current research at an August 1999 international meeting on alcoholism, states:

> With the neuroscience cooking along as it is, and the prospect that we'll find genes related to alcoholism, we would have far more targeted drug therapies for alcoholism in the next five to ten years.

A 1997 *Time* magazine article entitled "How We Get Addicted" discussed the generally accepted theory that addiction occurs because alcohol and drugs act on several important neurotransmitters and their receptors on brain cells, with both acute and long-term effects. Much of the research focuses on the elevation of a brain chemical called dopamine. Certain individuals, for reasons that are not totally understood, are more susceptible to this elevation than others. Even inherited genetic factors are no guarantee that you will or will not experience this effect. The simple fact is, one person will get hooked, another will not.

The Stages of the Disease

Although we still have much to learn about the causes of alcoholism and addiction, we do know a great deal about the progression from drugs and alcohol use to abuse to eventual dependency. We know how this happens, why it happens, and how this progression is harmful to abusers and their families. It is helpful to understand this process so as to be able to intervene sooner to prevent serious harm and, if one is a chronic addict/alcoholic, death.

Stage One: Learning About Mood-Altering Substances. The social use of alcohol is commonly accepted in our culture. In addition, many of us learned from our first experiences with alcohol that even one glass of wine or beer affects the way we feel, usually in a pleasant way. We learned, as promised in the many ads we see on television or on billboards, that we relaxed, lightened up, and enjoyed ourselves when we had a drink or two. We learned that the upward swing in our mood happened every time we drank, and that the degree of the swing increased the more we drank. In short, we learned the pleasurable effects of alcohol.

We also learned what happens when we drink more than we can handle. Our mood still continues in an upward swing, but, past a certain point, there are some unpleasant consequences as well. Those drinking too much might be embarrassed, for example, because their loud and talkative behavior or flushed cheeks reveal that they have had too much to drink. Others may become combative or even abusive when under the influence of alcohol or drugs. Some might feel sick the next day.

Stage Two: Seeking the Mood Swing. The discovery of the unpleasant effects of alcohol represents an important turning point that influences whether or not a person will go on to substance abuse. At this point, the negative effects are still reversible. The drinker can recover from one experience with embarrassment or a hangover, and next time, foregoes the greater upswing in mood in order to avoid the subsequent discomfort.

On the other hand, some drinkers decide the maximum high is worth whatever pain they experience as a result of exceeding their limit. They can also decide that the negative consequences can be rationalized away.

Two teens describe their different perceptions of the consequences of drinking:

> I get very light-headed when I drink, and I can feel it after just one beer. I don't like the feeling, and it keeps me from having a good time. So I stop with just one.

> I learned early that I can't tolerate alcohol, but I didn't care. The high was worth it. And when I kept drinking more, and did really stupid things, I rationalized that I had had a bad day at school or my parents were on my back too much. It didn't really matter that I had consequences. I liked using, and I wanted to continue with it no matter what anyone said. If negative things happened as a result, I just blamed outside forces for how I was acting.

Humans of any age can go through the denial, delusion, and rationalization process when seeking a mood swing with drugs or alcohol. Some, like the first teen, do not—they recognize unpleasant consequences as a signal that exceeding their limit is not in their best interest. Others, similar to the second teen, an alcoholic, focus on what drinking does *for* them and minimize the reality of what it does *to* them. Notice by what the alcoholic teen said that there is often a blaming of someone or something, such as parents or a bad day, to further justify the drinking behavior. There is also an element of self-pity that feeds the rationalization.

Rationalizing Addiction

Teen addicts who entered treatment and are now sober show further how chemical abusers and addicts think:

> My mom was on my case all the time, so I needed to get high with my friends just to get away from her. Of course I didn't want to admit to myself that she had a right to be on my case because of all the trouble I was in. I persuaded myself that I deserved to get high because she was such a witch.

> My parents were on my case all the time because I got in trouble once for showing up high at school. I kept doing it, but I just got better at hiding it. I rationalized that school was stupid, so it didn't matter if I was high when I got there.

> I was mad at my parents for sending me to a therapist so I thought it was fine that I lied to him about my drug use. Actually, I thought that my therapist was so stupid he couldn't tell the difference between a lie and the truth. That's what I focused on when I went to therapy. It was a joke to me.

> My friends and I thought that everyone in our community was too uptight, so it didn't matter that we did the vandalism we did. Anyway, we were high when we did it, and we just thought it was another good time.

As these addicts and alcoholics illustrate, denial, delusion, and rationalization, accompanied by self-pity, constitute the engine that moves the substance abuse and addiction process forward. In addition, those who are abusing drugs and alcohol have the sincere belief that their problems will go away if they can change other people, something they are doing, or something in their environment. This sincere belief, their self-delusion, traps them in their harmful progression. As this former teen addict explains, delusion goes with blindness:

> As I look back, I went to treatment totally convinced that I would show the treatment staff and my parents that I was not an addict. And I was really mad at my parents that they were taking me to this hospital to get help for something that wasn't even a problem. This was really hard for my parents because I had put them through hell. But I was so deluded, and I had

an excuse for everything that I was doing. When I started to work on my addiction, of course I saw how blind I really was. I look back now and see how powerful the disease really is. But the practicing addict can't see it.

Constant Pain

Stage Three: Harmful Abuse, Harmful Dependency. Those adolescents who keep abusing drugs and alcohol despite harmful consequences move further and further along the continuum of abuse to dependency. Even when they are sober, they are in pain. Their environment may be chaotic; they may not feel well physically; others may be angry with them; they may be racked with shame or sadness. They no longer use mood-altering chemicals to feel better than normal—they never even feel as good as normal used to feel. Now they are using to blot out the pain of their consequences. They keep using because their earlier experiences taught them that using drugs and alcohol made them feel good. Using used to work every time to elevate their mood.

During this stage of moving from harmful abuse to dependency, however, the emotional price for using mood-altering chemicals becomes greater. There is the delusion for addicts that they are moving in a positive direction. In fact, the consequences from using send them deeper into emotional—and often physical—pain.

A teen addict who is now sober relates how emotional pain worsens:

> As I look back, the simple solution to all my problems was just to use more often. I thought that I would feel better if I could just get more drugs. What a delusion. My progression got worse and worse and I had even more emotional pain as a result.

A treatment professional who has worked with adults and adolescents explains how deterioration and harmful abuse go together:

> When addicts enter treatment, they are deteriorating in all areas of their lives: socially, physically, emotionally, intellectually, and spiritually. Drugs and alcohol are being used to relieve guilt, fear, and anxiety about their consequences. They are more and more preoccupied with using drugs and alcohol to cover up these feelings. The pain goes deeper and deeper. There is the vicious cycle of using to cover up the pain, but then having to use because of it.

Stage Four: Chronic and Fatal Addiction. If addicts do not receive help for their addiction early on, it will progress to chronic dependency. Still deluded that drugs or alcohol will work *for* them, they use because they are in much pain, but in fact, they never move much beyond that low point. Their lives are falling apart, and deep within their psyche, they know it.

Blackouts are longer and more frequent, and there are many physical problems because addicts will often ignore their nutritional needs and their resistance to infection is low. There is a desperation to get high, often to prevent the pain of withdrawal. Suspicious thinking increases because of memory loss due to blackouts. At this stage, addicts/alcoholics usually have high anxiety about their behaviors and increased guilt. They feel helpless and hopeless. But, as an adult addict with many years of sobriety relates, they still want to keep using drugs and alcohol:

> When I went from being a graduate of Notre Dame with a highly successful career in radio to an alcoholic bum on the streets, I still believed that if only I could get another drink, my troubles would all go away.

Driven to Despair

This is the power of alcoholism and addiction. Addicts at this stage are very depressed and still undertake an often-futile search for another drink or drug to take the pain away. They may also decide that the best way to end their pain is to end their lives. Another adult who has been sober for years explains how pain can lead to death:

> Before I went to treatment the last time, I tried to hang myself in a cell when I was picked up for a DUI. I knew that my life was at a really low point, and I didn't think that there was any hope for me. When I read stories in the paper about people who succeed with suicide, I really feel sad. If only they could have gotten help like I did.

Evidence of the despair of chronic addicts is all around us if we look. Some citizens of Portland, Oregon, were reminded of the desperation in the chronic stage when they were driving home from work on July 1, 1998, and saw two bodies hanging from a steel bridge, twin nooses slipped around their necks. The couple in their 20s, Michael Douglas and fiancée Mora McGowan, were heroin addicts whose habit left them with unmanageable lives and no hope. Douglas left a journal that described their decision to end their lives.

The 1998 *Time* magazine article entitled "Public Suicide Awakens City to Problem of Drug Addiction" describes this event, focusing on the couple's despair:

> Those who knew Douglas said that drugs were always part of his life. When he and McGowan began using heroin, they started pawning everything they owned of any value to feed their habit. They were eventually kicked out of the friend's apartment where they had been staying and put on the streets.

> At least once, McGowan tried treatment but failed. In despair, she tried suicide by cutting her wrists, but her mother rushed

her to a hospital. Douglas tried to come up with the money to buy enough heroin for an overdose, but he couldn't.

Police Sgt. Kent Perry said Douglas wrote in his journal about the grind of having to raise $200 every day to pay for his fix and how he considered other ways of ending his life, including shooting himself or lying down on train tracks.

This story shows how much despair exists in chronic addicts. It also summarizes the disease model of addiction and illustrates the co-existence of drug dependency and other psychiatric disorders such as depression and suicidal thinking. Drug dependency was primary, progressive, chronic, and fatal in those young persons' lives.

Substance abuse can progress to dependency if it is not stopped. The illness can become chronic and end with addicts taking their own lives. Fatalities can also occur from acts of poor judgment such as accidental overdoses and automobile and boating accidents. The daily newspaper is filled with stories of such needless deaths.

Adolescent Brains Are More Prone to Addiction

Associated Press

The following selection from the Associated Press examines recent research into the connection between adolescent brain development and addiction. According to researchers, the adolescent brain is still developing, especially in the region that controls priority-setting, planning, and the inhibition of impulses. Because this area of the brain is not fully developed, researchers believe, teens are more prone than adults to take risks, such as experimenting with addictive substances. Additionally, scientists have found that exposure to drugs and alcohol during this period of adolescent brain development can damage the parts of the brain associated with addiction, creating a more intense reaction to addictive substances. The Associated Press provides news stories for major news organizations around the world.

Every parent dreads it.

Almost overnight a sweet, cheerful, obedient child mutates into a churlish monster prone to recklessness and unpredictable mood swings.

This is not *The Exorcist*. This is adolescence.

Parents and experts always have blamed the same hormones that catapult young bodies into adulthood for the sleeping until noon, the reckless driving, the drug use and the other woes of adolescence. But recent research shows that what's going on above teen-agers' necks, not raging hormones, explains the changes.

Beginning around age 11, the brain undergoes major reorganization in an area associated with things such as social behavior and impulse control. Neuroscientists figured this out only in the past few years, and the discovery has led them to see adolescence as a period when the developing brain is vulnerable to traumatic experiences, drug abuse and unhealthy influences.

"The adolescent brain is different. It's still growing," said Fulton Crews, a neuroscientist at the University of North Carolina at Chapel Hill.

Reprinted by permission of the Associated Press from "It's All in Teens' Heads: Changing Brains Cause Tumult of Adolescence," wire story of January 5, 2001.

Brain Growth Continues Through Adolescence

Not long ago, neuroscientists thought the brain stopped growing by the time a child entered nursery school. By then, it was thought, nearly all the brain's wiring had been connected and the only remaining task was to program that hardware.

But new brain imaging technologies have shattered that notion. Using techniques like magnetic resonance imaging (MRI) and positron emission tomography, or PET scanning, researchers have detected brain growth throughout childhood and well into adolescence.

Because their brains are not yet mature, adolescents do not handle social pressure, instinctual urges and other stresses the way adults do. That may explain in part why adolescents are so prone to unsavory or reckless behavior.

"The adolescent brain is just in a different state than the adult brain," Crews said.

Researchers in the scientific journal *Nature* presented a series of time-lapse images depicting brain growth from age 3 to 15. The images showed a tangle of nerve cells sprouting in the part of the brain that sits above the eyes, then a period of "pruning" after puberty, when about half of the new fibers are cut away to create an efficient network of circuits.

All this action happens in a part of the brain known as the prefrontal cortex, an area responsible for what neuroscientists call the "executive functions." Those functions are practically a laundry list of the qualities adolescents often lack—goal-setting, priority-setting, planning, organization and impulse inhibition.

Adolescence is a time of risk-taking, said Lynn Ponton, a psychiatrist at the University of California, San Francisco, and author of *The Romance of Risk: Why Teen-agers Do the Things They Do.*

"A big part of adolescence is learning how to assess the risk in an activity," Ponton said. "Part of the reason teen-agers aren't good at risk-taking is that the brain isn't fully developed."

Looked at that way, it is no big surprise that accidents are the leading cause of death among adolescents, or that teens are more likely to become crime victims than any other age group. It's no wonder the vast majority of alcoholics and smokers get started during their teen years, or that a quarter of all people with HIV contract it before age 21.

Adolescent Experiences Determine Adult Behavior

It's no secret that things such as criminal records and sexually transmitted diseases can really mess up a life. But neuroscientists are learning that less serious things can have lasting effects, too.

Scientists conduct most of their research on adolescent brain development using animals, because it would be unethical to experiment with human teens. Animals don't all go through a transitional period between childhood and adulthood, but most mammals do exhibit some kind of adolescence.

"They don't hang out at malls and spike their hair and stuff, but their social behavior and social structure changes dramatically," said Linda Spear of Binghamton University in New York state.

Adolescent rats, for example, show more interest than adults do when strange objects are put in their cages. They start hanging out with their peers more, exploring their surroundings intensely and flitting from one activity to the next.

Craig Ferris, who studies golden hamsters at the University of Massachusetts Medical Center in Worcester, said that in the wild his study subjects enter adolescence when they are ejected from the nest at about 25 days of age. For about two weeks they wander through wheat fields, looking for a nest that will take them in or founding one of their own.

Ferris' experiments show that a golden hamster's experiences during this stage can determine how it will behave for the rest of its life. If an adolescent golden hamster is put in a cage with an aggressive adult for an hour each day, it will grow up to become a bully that picks on animals smaller than itself. But it will cower in fear around hamsters its own size.

Those golden hamsters raised in the presence of aggressive adults also grow up to have lower-than-normal levels of vasopressin, a chemical associated with aggression, in the brain's hypothalamus. They also sprout more receptors in the hypothalamus for serotonin, a chemical that blocks vasopressin.

Ferris and his colleagues aren't sure exactly what to make of the chemical changes they observe. But they are certain that at least for golden hamsters, being intimidated by an adult during adolescence has permanent effects.

"The take-home of all this stuff is that the brain is constantly interacting with the environment," Ferris said.

During adolescence, Ferris and his colleagues hypothesize, the developing brain picks up cues from the environment and uses them to help determine "normal" behavior.

"If the environment provokes or encourages aberrant behaviors, those behaviors become the norm," said Jordan Grafman of the National Institute of Neurological Diseases and Stroke.

Adolescent Brains and Addiction

To neuroscientists, one of the most disturbing behaviors among adolescents is binge drinking. Studies already have shown that alcohol exposure in utero can have devastating effects on the developing brain, and many researchers fear that the period of vulnerability could extend through childhood and into adolescence.

Researchers at the University of North Carolina recently decided to test the sensitivity of the adolescent brain to binge drinking by subjecting rats to an alcohol binge. Four times a day for four days, they gave adolescent and adult rats 10 grams of alcohol per kilogram of body weight. After the rats had sobered up, the researchers looked for brain damage and found more in adolescent rats than in adults. Most important, the adolescents sustained damage in brain regions associated with addiction.

"My hypothesis is that this damage is a component of the development of alcoholism," Crews said.

Researchers who study cigarette smoking tell a similar story. The vast majority of smokers start during their teen years, but until recently nobody had thought to look at how the adolescent brain responds to nicotine.

When they did, researchers at Duke University found that adolescent brains respond more intensely to nicotine. The scientists injected rats with nicotine every day for more than two weeks, a dose comparable to what a typical smoker receives. In all of the rats the number of chemical receptors dedicated to nicotine increased—a sign of addiction. But in adolescents, the number of nicotine receptors increased twice as much compared with adults.

"What we found is that the adolescent brain gets a lot more bang for the buck," said Theodore Slotkin, one of the researchers.

A follow-up study published in the October 2000 issue of *Brain Research* showed that adolescent nicotine exposure caused permanent behavioral problems as well, especially for females. Even after two weeks with no nicotine, female rats were less interested in moving around and raising their young than counterparts who had never been exposed.

That may be because nicotine retards cell division in the hippocampus, a brain region that continues growing into adulthood in females, but not males.

It also may be that the nicotine-exposed rats were depressed. Nicotine decreases the brain's production of norepinephrin and dopamine, two chemicals that tend to be lower in depressed people. And epidemiological studies have shown that smoking early in life greatly increases a person's chances of suffering depression later on.

That doesn't mean that people who begin smoking at a young age are doomed to live out their days depressed and in thrall to nicotine.

"A person isn't a slave to one's genes or biology," Ferris said.

But even at this early stage of research, he added, it is clear that things like violence and drugs can permanently alter a teen-ager's brain. And that may make an often difficult period even tougher.

TOBACCO ADVERTISING INTENTIONALLY TARGETS TEENS

Infact

In the following selection, the corporate watchdog group Infact discusses the tactics used by tobacco companies to attract teenagers to cigarettes. Because the tobacco industry loses nearly five thousand customers every day, Infact maintains, the tobacco companies desperately need teens to develop the habit of smoking. To this end, the companies employ tactics that appeal to teens, such as the use of cartoon characters as spokespeople, free cigarette giveaways at teen hangouts, and sponsorship of rock concerts and sporting events. Furthermore, Infact writes, tobacco companies offer promotional merchandise—including sunglasses and backpacks—that appeals strongly to teens. According to Infact, the result of these strategies has been an increase in young smokers in the United States and around the world. Founded in 1977, Infact is a national organization headquartered in Boston, Massachusetts.

The tobacco industry loses close to 5,000 customers every day in the US alone—including 3,500 who manage to quit and about 1,200 who die. The most promising "replacement smokers" are young people: 90% of smokers begin before they're 21, and 60% before they're 14! To find their new customers, *every day* US tobacco companies spend $11 million to advertise and promote cigarettes—more than the US Federal Office on Smoking and Health spends to prevent smoking in an *entire year*.

American Youth: "Cool" Customers

In the US, cigarette advertising links smoking with being "cool," taking risks, and growing up. At the same time the tobacco industry insists that it does not want children to smoke—and backs up its claims with campaigns supposedly designed to discourage young people from smoking. But programs like "Tobacco: Helping Youth Say No" are not only slick public relations efforts designed to bolster

Reprinted, with permission, from "Tobacco Marketing to Young People," fact sheet from Infact's tobacco industry campaign, available at www.infact.org/youth.html.

industry credibility, they actually *encourage* youth tobacco use. By leaving out the health dangers, ignoring addiction, and glamorizing smoking as an "adult custom," these campaigns reinforce the industry's advertising theme presenting smoking as a way for children to exert independence and be grown up.

Outside the US, central messages are wealth, health, consumption—in short, "USA." According to Kenyan physician Paul Wangai, "Many African children have two hopes. One is to go to heaven, the other to America. US tobacco companies capitalize on this by associating smoking with affluence. It's not uncommon to hear children say they start because of the glamorous life-style associated with smoking."

In emerging markets from Eastern Europe to Southeast Asia, transnational tobacco giants Philip Morris, RJR Nabisco, and BAT Industries aggressively hawk cigarettes with slogans like "L & M: The Way America Tastes," "Winston: The Spirit of the USA," and "Lucky Strikes: An American Original." These themes, and the images that accompany them, expand the appeal of this deadly product beyond what has in many countries been an adult male market to young people and women.

Marketing Tobacco to Teens

Some promotional tactics proven effective in reaching young people around the world include the use of cartoon images, free cigarette giveaways, sponsorship of events that especially appeal to young people, and the use of cigarette logos on youth-oriented products.

RJR Nabisco's Joe Camel campaign is a particularly appalling example of the industry hitting its target. Modeled after James Bond and Don Johnson of *Miami Vice*, Joe Camel has profoundly influenced even the very young. One study showed that nearly one-third of three-year-olds matched Joe Camel with cigarettes and that by age six, children were as familiar with him as with the Mickey Mouse logo on the Disney Channel! The cartoon Camel catapulted Camel cigarettes from a brand smoked by less than 1% of US smokers under age 18 to a one-third share of the youth market—and nearly one-half billion dollars in annual sales—within three years.

The enormous success of Joe Camel has apparently inspired other cartoon ad campaigns, including a penguin tested by Brown & Williamson, US subsidiary of transnational giant BAT Industries. "Willie the Kool," the penguin used to promote Kool cigarettes, has buzz-cut hair, day-glo sneakers, sunglasses, and is very conscious of being "cool."

With an addictive product, it doesn't take much to hook a new customer. For the tobacco companies, the expense of giving away free samples is dwarfed by the potential for long-term gains—especially from new young customers.

• Young women in "cowgirl" outfits hand out free Philip Morris

Marlboros to teenagers at rock concerts and discos in Eastern Europe. Those who accept a light on the spot are rewarded with Marlboro sunglasses. The world's leading cigarette brand, Marlboro was the number one cigarette among US teenagers long before it dominated the market overall.

• High school students in Taipei flood the Whisky A Go-Go disco, where free packs of RJR Nabisco Salems are on each table.

• At a high school in Buenos Aires, a woman wearing khaki safari gear and driving a jeep with the yellow Camel logo hands out free cigarettes to 15- and 16-year-olds on their lunch recess.

Tobacco companies gain widespread exposure for their brands and associate their deadly products with positive experiences by sponsoring a wide variety of events around the world. Rock concerts and sporting events in particular reach large audiences of young people.

Rock concerts, with their celebrity stars, Western image, and enormous following of young fans, have been a magnet for tobacco industry sponsorship outside the US. In countries where cigarette advertising is banned or restricted, sponsoring live or televised concerts enables the companies to get around local regulations.

• In Taiwan, RJR Nabisco agents arranged a concert by teen idol Hsow-Yu Chang, with five empty packs of Winstons the only accepted admission "ticket"—ten for a souvenir sweatshirt.

• Among the performances sponsored by RJR's Salem were a live concert by Paula Abdul in Seoul and a televised concert by Madonna in Hong Kong—where TV ads for tobacco are banned. Also in Hong Kong, Philip Morris sponsored the Marlboro Rock-In, a series of televised concerts.

Sports sponsorship is especially insidious, because it implies that smoking and fitness mix. Young people seeing cigarette logos linked with their heroes, excitement, speed, and triumph are likely to lose sight of the reality of death, disease, and addiction. In the US, companies receive valuable television air time by sponsoring sports, and evade the federal ban on television advertising of tobacco.

• Philip Morris's Virginia Slims tennis and RJR Nabisco's Winston Cup auto racing were both launched in 1971—the same year the federal law barring cigarette ads from television and radio took effect.

• During the 1989 Indianapolis 500, Marlboro received over $2.6 million worth of advertising exposure.

Another clever way to keep cigarette brands constantly in the public eye and circumvent restrictions on advertising is known as "brand stretching"—using cigarette logos on other products. Many of these products are fun and fashionable for children in the US and around the world, who become walking billboards for tobacco. US promotions in particular often have the added danger of rewarding cigarette consumption by offering merchandise in exchange for coupons from cigarette packs.

• RJR built on the Joe Camel campaign in 1991 with the "Camel Cash" promotion, offering coupons resembling one-dollar bills in every pack of filtered Camel cigarettes. These "Camel C-notes" picture Joe Camel, in sunglasses and smoking, dressed as George Washington. Consumers can redeem Camel Cash for "smooth stuff" with obvious appeal to young people—"flip-flops," insulators for beverage cans, jackets, towels, T-shirts, and hats—all featuring Joe Camel.

• Philip Morris offers nine items, including black leather back-packs, a tough biker jacket, sunglasses, and vests, in its new Virginia Slims "V-Wear" line. According to a Philip Morris marketing vice president, "Fashion has always been an element with Virginia Slims."

• Children are given Marlboro T-shirts in Kenya, and Marlboro clothing in Guatemala.

• In Thailand, cigarette logos have appeared on kites, T-shirts, pants, notebooks, earrings, and chewing gum packages.

• In Kuala Lumpur, Malaysia, a record store called the Salem Power Station wraps customers' tapes in advertisements for Salem cigarettes. Nearby, a Camel Adventure Gear store sells Camel brand products.

The Results: Youth Smoking on the Rise

After declining every year for 25 years, US smoking rates increased slightly in 1991—reflecting the tobacco industry's success at hooking young smokers. More than 3,000 US teens become regular smokers *each day*, with girls smoking at a higher rate than boys.

• Since RJR's Joe Camel campaign began, smoking among US teens is up 10%.

• US teenagers buy the most heavily promoted cigarettes, and 80% of teens consider advertising influential in encouraging them to begin to smoke.

• The tobacco industry began aggressively targeting women with Philip Morris's introduction of Virginia Slims in 1968. Within six years, the number of teenage girls smoking more than doubled.

Transnational tobacco companies such as Philip Morris, RJR Nabisco, BAT Industries, and American Brands are also making their presence felt in other countries. In the developing world, per capita cigarette consumption has risen on average by more than 70% during the last 25 years.

• Hong Kong children as young as seven years old are addicted to cigarettes.

• The teen smoking rate in some Latin American cities is 50%.

• In Kenya, the smoking rate among primary school children was estimated at 40% in 1989—a huge jump from the 10% level estimated a decade earlier.

• Smoking rates among male Korean teenagers rose from 18% to 30% in one year after the entry of US tobacco companies. Among female teenagers, rates increased from less than 2% to nearly 9%.

THE WIDESPREAD GAMBLING CULTURE MAY PROMOTE ADDICTION IN TEENS

Virginia Young and Kim Bell

Recent studies have found that more and more teens are becoming addicted to gambling. In the following selection, Virginia Young and Kim Bell discuss the link between teen gambling and the pervasiveness of gambling in society. For example, they write, many games found at video arcades and gaming palaces are designed to emulate the games of chance found in casinos. Drawn by the possibility of winning prizes, children and teens become familiar with these games and may progress to the actual casino games later on. In addition, parents have become more likely to buy scratch-off lottery tickets for teens or even younger children. The authors also note that many young people are able to circumvent laws designed to prevent teen access to casinos, lotteries, and sports betting. This easy access to the culture of gambling seems to be a contributing factor to the rise in problem gambling among teenagers, they conclude. Young and Bell are staff writers for the *St. Louis Post-Dispatch*.

Nearly 6 percent of teen-agers younger than 18 have serious gambling problems, a study says. Those who have problems are likely to miss school and use alcohol and drugs. Fueling it all, some experts say, is that gambling has become socially acceptable and that children sometimes are enticed—in the company of their parents—to take a chance.

Adolescents are betting on sports contests and private card games. They're buying lottery tickets and trying to sneak into casinos.

Nearly 6 percent of teen-agers under 18 have serious gambling problems compared with slightly more than 1 percent of the adult population, a national study says.

Researchers at Harvard School of Medicine came up with the figures by synthesizing estimates from 120 gambling studies in the United States and Canada. The results were reported in the September 1999 *American Journal of Public Health*.

While adults with gambling problems may ruin their marriages and amass credit card debt, youths with gambling problems are likely to miss school and use alcohol and drugs.

"Many times, all the risky behaviors are coupled together," says Marilyn Bader, who works on prevention efforts for the National Council on Alcohol and Drug Abuse in the St. Louis area. "They might be playing cards and smoking and drinking."

Gambling Is Socially Acceptable

Why are kids gambling?

They're growing up in an era in which gambling is socially accepted. Lottery tickets are given to them as presents, churches run raffles, charities promote bingo, and casinos are springing up in the nation's heartland.

"We believe there's no coincidence with what we're seeing," says Laura Letson, executive director of the New York Council on Problem Gambling. "They're frankly just mirroring adults and the message they're getting from society.

"You can go to a supermarket and observe a parent teaching a 2-year-old how to scratch off a lottery ticket. If the parent was teaching them how to drink a bottle of beer, society would be absolutely appalled."

Research indicates that children are more likely to gamble if their parents gamble. And the National Gambling Impact Study Commission reported in 1999 that individuals who begin gambling at an early age run a higher risk of developing a gambling problem.

No one has determined whether there's any connection between such problems and the hours today's youths spend playing video and arcade games. But the pastime may provide fodder for future studies.

"It isn't a great leap from any type of video game to video poker," says Glenn R. McGowan, who counsels problem gamblers in south St. Louis County, Missouri.

From Games to Gambling

Although barred from casinos until age 21, children can accompany their parents to Dave & Buster's, a high-tech restaurant and game palace in Maryland Heights, Missouri. Owned by a Dallas chain, the restaurant is within sight of the tower of the Riverport Casino Center.

At Dave & Buster's, patrons use electronic cards to play the machines and store their tickets in a cardboard "Big Winner's Cup." T-shirts, stuffed animals and radios are among the prizes.

Games such as Pokereno have obvious poker themes. Twenty One, in which the player rolls a ball into holes marked by numbers, teaches children the combinations of numbers they need to reach 21.

Cash Roulette and Hi-Roller are similar to a game found in Vegas casinos. Players at Dave & Buster's drop a gold token down a chute. (In Vegas, adults drop quarters or silver dollars.) A spinning wheel spits it onto a ledge with piles of other tokens. If the player's token lands just right, it will force other tokens off the edge and into the winner's tray.

"It was easy," says Samantha Steimel, 11, as she waits in line to redeem 1,653 tickets. "Me and my Dad won these."

Nearby, Austin Schuttner celebrates his sixth birthday playing Lite a Line, where he rolled a ball down a table into holes marked by numbers. With each winning combination of numbers, the machine spits out more yellow tickets to be redeemed for prizes. Austin is so small that his grandmother, Jeri Harlan of High Ridge, Missouri, lets him sit on the machine so he can see his targets.

Harlan dismisses a question about whether such games train kids for adult casinos.

"The children don't know about Vegas," she says. "It's just a lot of fun. They enjoy picking out their own gifts. Austin got over 2,000 tickets, and he got a *Star Wars* watch with Darth Vader on it and some Pokemon stickers."

The owners say the business is geared toward adults. Its brochures include no pictures of children. The company isn't trying to woo youngsters or train gamblers, said Reggie Moultrie, the company's vice president of amusement.

"Children should be within arm's length of the parent, and if a parent doesn't feel (the games) are appropriate, we don't want them around it," Moultrie said. "It's the parents' call on whether it's open and accessible."

Machines that meet criteria spelled out in a 1984 St. Louis County court case are banned and can be seized. Among the criteria: Money must be inserted to play, the game's outcome depends on chance and the machines keep track of points and clear credits for the next player.

Moultrie said all of his games are legal. He said his company consulted a former FBI forensic specialist, who concluded the games required enough skill to make them legal. With High Roller, for example, the person dropping the token down a chute can position a chute to direct the token.

"Each of the games has a trick or skill method that will allow you to get better each time," Moultrie said. "To the naked eye, it would look like the games are exactly the same (as in Vegas), but at Dave & Buster's we make sure they're games of skill so we comply with all local ordinances."

Dave & Buster's may be the most sophisticated, but plenty of places offer similar reward-oriented games for children.

Swing Around Fun Town in Fenton, Missouri, is geared toward families and plays host to children's birthday parties most weekends. Kathy Reuther, an owner, says children can win tickets on some games and redeem them for prizes.

"I don't really look at it that it has any twist on gambling," she says. "I don't think the children play the games for the points. They come in there for the sheer entertainment. Like joining a baseball team, they want to win. They do it for competitiveness, to make themselves better, faster, sharper."

Reuther also argues that the redemption games, "believe it or not, have an educational value. If a child has 100 points, he'll actually stand there and decide how to best spend the 100 points. Will he buy two or three things? Or save up his points and come back another time?"

Teens Get Around Gambling Laws

Some teens try to get into casinos, but the industry says it aggressively enforces the law against underage bettors.

Harrah's "Project 21" handbook teaches employees what types of identification cards are acceptable and how to look for other cues that a person's age should be closely checked.

In 1999, 282 minors were arrested on Missouri riverboats for presenting false IDs. Customers must show IDs to get electronic boarding passes.

The Missouri Lottery warns its vendors to ask anyone for identification who looks younger than 18. A few retailers have had their licenses pulled for selling to minors.

Studies of lottery sales in other states suggest it's easy to get around the age rules.

The Illinois State Crime Commission found that two girls, ages 12 and 14, had no trouble buying lottery tickets in 1996 from vending machines. The girls succeeded 20 out of 20 times. Three years earlier, a study published in the *Journal of Gambling Studies* found that a girl, 16, was able to buy lottery tickets from 49 of 50 central Illinois retailers.

In New York, nearly one-third of the adolescents surveyed by Rachel Volberg of Gemini Research said they had been able to purchase lottery tickets. Overall, 2.4 percent of New York adolescents age 13 to 17 were experiencing severe difficulties because of gambling. That adds up to 41,000 teen-agers.

At colleges, sports betting is the main worry. Every campus has student bookies, an NCAA official has said, even though it's illegal in all but two states.

The NCAA has asked Congress to ban sports betting, which would affect Nevada and Oregon. Nevada allows betting on professional and amateur sports, while the Oregon Lottery runs a game involving pro football games.

Backers of such a ban say sports gambling in Nevada legitimizes and promotes illegal sports wagering on college campuses.

The proposal has brought out the heavy artillery from the gambling industry, which says the bill unfairly targets Nevada, cannot be enforced and ignores the problem of illegal gambling outside of Nevada.

The St. Louis Post-Dispatch, like most newspapers, publishes sports betting odds.

"The line does provide information in terms of who is favored, and by how much—and we have trained our readers over many years to expect this information," said Managing Editor Arnie Robbins.

Do Teen Gamblers Become Adult Gamblers?

One of the authorities on youth gambling, Ken Winters of the University of Minnesota, says that while the rate of problem gambling among youths is "provocatively high," it might not be quite so bad as it sounds.

Pathological gambling hits adults like a tornado, devastating their finances, careers and families. With teens, who have less money to lose, the key question is whether they are sowing the seeds for a problem later in life. That's the focus of Winters' current research.

A clinical psychologist and associate professor in the university's Department of Psychiatry, he is tracking a group of young adults first interviewed as adolescents. He's finding that many outgrow their gambling problems, just as people reduce their alcohol consumption as they move into careers and child-rearing roles.

He's still curious to see how youths who grew up on video games will react to the new generation of slot machines being developed. Casinos are making the machines faster and adding joysticks to appeal to the younger market, he says.

In schools, students already are warned about the risks of drugs, premarital sex and drunken driving. Some states have begun adding gambling warnings to the mixture.

The national gambling study commission singled out Minnesota for leading the way with a program that includes posters targeted toward adolescents and speakers who lecture on the risks of gambling. Minnesota has 16 casinos on tribal land.

Youths can gamble when they turn 18. Many can't wait.

"Up here, they like to get there on midnight of their birthday," says Roger Svendsen, director of gambling programs for the nonprofit Minnesota Institute of Public Health. That's how his son celebrated his 18th birthday.

Getting the Message to Teens

Svendsen says his message to students is simple: Set limits. He tells them that low-risk gambling is done purely for fun or recreation— "never to make money. I've said that in front of college students and they look at you like you're crazy."

New York officials hope to start getting that point across to elementary, middle and high school students in a pilot project. State education officials and the New York Council on Problem Gambling Inc. formed a think tank that is developing ways to include the information in the public schools' curriculum.

A study at the University of Mississippi says it may be possible to "inoculate" children against the dangers of gambling at an early age, "so that they approach risk-taking opportunities with skepticism."

The researchers asked 5- and 6-year-olds to pay a dime to play a game. While blindfolded, the children selected colored chips from a cup. Depending on the color chosen, they would get their dime back, double their money, lose the dime or win a big stuffed animal (a 1-in-16 chance). Candy was later substituted for dimes, since it was more valuable to the children.

The trials were fixed so that the children accumulated three dimes or candies at two points in the game but ran out of currency if they played 20 times. They could stop at any time. One week later, they were given the same opportunity.

Among the findings, reported in the *Journal of Gambling Studies* in 1998: Children were more likely to quit while they were ahead the second time, suggesting that they recognized the low chance of winning the big prize.

Another study from 1998 indicated that parents should be educated, too. Canadian researchers found that most parents underestimated the extent of youth gambling and the problems it can cause.

PARENTAL LENIENCE CAN LEAD TO TEEN ADDICTION

Donna Leinwand

As unlikely as it may seem, Donna Leinwand reports in the following article, the parents of some teenagers do not completely prohibit drug use by their children. According to Leinwand, these parents believe their children are going to experiment with drugs regardless of any warnings; therefore, they prefer to allow their teens to use drugs at home under their supervision rather than out on the streets. However, the author warns, this strategy often backfires as these teens quickly become addicted. In a few cases, Leinwand reveals, parents have shared drugs with their children—or even introduced their teens to illegal drugs— without realizing the harm they were doing. Leinwand is a staff writer for *USA Today*.

They are scenes that paint a startling picture of the drug culture's legacy on American home life: A teenage girl shares her hopes and dreams with her mother—as they binge on methamphetamines. A boy bonds with his father over a marijuana-filled bong.

For the vast majority of families, scenes such as these are hard to fathom. But counselors who deal with teen addicts across the USA say that parents' complicity has become a significant factor in putting kids on a path to drug dependency.

A survey in 2000 of nearly 600 teens in drug treatment in New York, Texas, Florida and California indicated that 20% have shared drugs other than alcohol with their parents, and that about 5% of the teens actually were introduced to drugs—usually marijuana—by their moms or dads.

The survey follows a report from 1999 by the Partnership for a Drug-Free America in which 8% of teens in the overall population who said they had been offered drugs indicated that at least some of the offers came from a parent.

Parents Are Enabling Teen Drug Users

Classmates or neighborhood friends remain far and away the most likely sources of drugs for teens. But counselors say the latest survey documents a troubling trend: Some baby boomers who came of age as the drug culture exploded in the '60s and '70s are enablers for their children who experiment with drugs.

"I don't think we're at the peak of it yet," says David Rosenker, vice president of adolescent services at the Caron Foundation, a treatment program in Wernersville, Pa., that sees 6,000 kids a year. "We already see it a lot: baby boomer parents who are still using and still having a problem with their use. They're buying for their kids, smoking pot with their kids, using heroin with their kids.

"When I started (working with youths) in the mid-'70s, this was not happening."

Addiction specialists say it is happening now because of a range of factors that show how the rise in recreational drug use has altered traditional parent-child relationships, regardless of families' race or economic status:

• A small percentage of boomer parents have never given up drugs, and so their children see drug use and addiction as normal.

• Some parents believe that sharing an occasional joint with their teenager can ease family tensions and make a parent seem more like a buddy in whom their teen can confide. Parents also might view it as an easy way to explain their own past drug use.

• Other parents regard marijuana use as a relatively harmless rite of passage for young adults. It was for boomers; almost 60% of those born in the USA from 1946 through 1964 say they have smoked pot at some point in their lives, a Partnership survey found in 1999. But since boomers' days of rebellion, the drug landscape has changed. A smaller percentage of youths are using drugs regularly, but marijuana and other drugs are more potent than ever, and first-time users are more likely to be in middle school than in college.

• Many parents—75% in the Partnership survey—say they believe that most people will try illegal drugs at some point. Some parents, counselors say, naively figure that they're "protecting" their kids by allowing or even encouraging some drug use in the home.

"Do It at Home"

Pamela Straub, 43, of Whittier, Calif., developed a drug habit in junior high school. So when her own daughter, Felicia Nunnink, discovered her stash of marijuana in a living room cabinet, Straub decided to lay down some rules.

"I just didn't want her out on the streets," says Straub, whose own drug use left her addicted to a range of drugs and homeless at one point. "I told her I'd rather have her do it at home where I could keep an eye on her. I smoked pot with Felicia. I can't really say if I was right or wrong. Well, now I guess I'm pretty sure I was wrong."

Straub says she has been drug-free for more than five years.

Nunnink, now 22, looks back fondly to her teenage days when she shared joints with her mother. Mellowed by the marijuana, she says she felt close to her, and they talked—more like friends than mother and daughter.

"At the time, I wanted to do it because I thought it was the only way to get a bond with my mom," says Nunnink, who moved on to methamphetamines, which she and her mother also shared. "It was cool. My house was where the kids came over to get high."

But Nunnink soon found she couldn't stop taking drugs. Now she's in rehabilitation and is thinking about what she would tell children she might have someday about drugs. "I would be very open with my kids about drugs and what they did to me. It really messed up my life," she says. "I think it's a bad idea even to smoke pot in front of kids."

Counselors say that Straub's actions, however well-meaning, show how parents can blur the boundaries between childhood and adulthood, sowing confusion for teens.

"We have 35 years of drug culture now," says Mitchell Rosenthal, president of the Phoenix House drug treatment program in New York, which conducted the 2000 study of teen addicts.

Rosenthal says he commissioned the study after speaking with three California teens who had used drugs with their parents. Phoenix House arranged for *USA Today* to discuss the study with several teens in its program.

"Many people who experimented with drugs in their own adolescence may be regular users, and many of them have children," he says. "Parents who do not set limits and who try to be buddies with their kids are doing their kids a real disservice. Kids have to be helped to control their impulses. They are not helped by parents who want to jump into the playpen."

Parents Set the Standard

On the flip side, parents can be a huge influence in steering a child from drugs, says Steve Dnistrian, executive vice president of the Partnership for a Drug-Free America. "You have perhaps the most drug-savvy group of parents ever," he says. "They have been there and done that, and they do not want their kids using drugs. But we have a disconnect.

"Most of them have a difficulty knowing what to say persuasively on this issue," Dnistrian says. "Dare the question come up: 'Mom, Dad, did you get high?' So you avoid it. You don't deal with it. Then someone else deals with it for you by offering your kids drugs."

Dnistrian recommends honesty. Tell your children what you learned from the past and set high expectations for them, he advises.

"If you are trying to establish expectations for your teenagers to meet, and you lower those expectations yourself by essentially giving them a green light to drink or smoke pot in your house, then you're really pulling the rug out from under yourself," Dnistrian says. "Parents who say their kids are going to smoke and drink anyway so they may as well do it here—that's like setting the standard at 'C.' So don't be surprised if they come home and tell you they've snorted cocaine or dropped acid. You've opened the door."

Although the Phoenix House survey covers only teens who already have gotten into trouble with drugs, Dnistrian says it underscores the vulnerability of children in families that use drugs.

"It tells you how ingrained substance abuse is in the family structure," he says. "These parents are so familiar with it and so close to it that they are willing to pass the joint to their children. This is something we have to watch."

Blurring Traditional Roles

In hindsight, Jason, 17, a recovering addict from an upper-middle-class family in Simi Valley, Calif., says he wishes his father had been more of a parent and less of a buddy when it came to marijuana.

Jason, whose last name is being withheld because he is a juvenile, says he first tried pot in the sixth grade with some classmates. He managed to hide signs of his drug use from his parents, who regularly attended his hockey games, scheduled family outings and vacations and kept tabs on his schoolwork.

Then he made his first drug purchase: a $5 bag of pot. Jason says his father walked by his room's open door as he was stashing it in a dresser drawer.

"He told me about his marijuana use," Jason says. "We went into his office, and he had a (water pipe) and we got high together. I thought he was *sooo* cool."

They began smoking together once a week.

"I felt a bond between me and my father when we were getting high," Jason says. "It's like a father-son experience. I had a warmth inside me like, 'My dad, he's cool. I love him.' We would talk about life."

Jason says his father told him that a little marijuana would be OK if he kept up his grades, played sports, avoided fights and practiced safe sex. His father condemned other drugs and despised Jason's cigarette habit, the teen says.

"He wouldn't see a problem with marijuana if you could handle your priorities," Jason says.

But Jason couldn't. He started smoking pot almost every day. He began defying teachers, ditching school and skipping hockey practice. "I was taking our household pets and selling them for money for drugs," says Jason, now in drug treatment at a Phoenix House in Orange County, Calif. "I took my brother's 3-foot iguana and sold it for a bag of weed. That's low."

Jason says marijuana "didn't interfere in any way with (his father's) life. It did mine. I guess the addicted gene skipped him and hit me." Contacted by officials at Phoenix House, Jason's parents confirmed his story but declined to comment further.

This isn't Jason's first shot at getting clean. He spent his 14th birthday in drug treatment, his 15th at a boot camp for troubled youths, his 16th in a group home and his 17th at Phoenix House. He wants to spend his 18th birthday like a typical teenager.

Looking back, he wishes his parents had tightened the reins earlier.

"Kids want parents to be friends," he says. "Parents need to realize it's more beneficial in the long run for parents to be parents. There are enough people outside telling us that things that are not OK are OK. Parents should be a safety zone."

A Family's Cycle of Addiction

In a few families, drug use has been passed on as though it were a tradition.

LaKiesha, 15, of Southern California, is the third generation of a family in which members have become addicted to drugs. LaKiesha says her grandmother smoked pot regularly and gave her a few puffs when she was 5 years old, to settle her down before bedtime.

LaKiesha's mother, Latricia, 32, says that while growing up she never thought of marijuana as a drug. She says her mother was a church-going licensed nurse who made sure the rent was paid and food was in the pantry, and who saw marijuana as "a natural herb." Their surname is being withheld because LaKiesha is a juvenile.

"My mother didn't look at it as a problem or addiction," Latricia says. "She felt as long as I was doing things at home, I was out of harm's way."

But the marijuana launched steep, parallel declines for Latricia and her daughter that landed both of them in rehabilitation.

"They say marijuana is a gateway drug, and it can be," says LaKiesha, who eventually moved on to PCP and alcohol abuse. "Marijuana was for the days I wanted to come down."

LaKiesha says she stopped smoking and drinking 11 months ago. Her mother, now a counselor, has been clean for five years. Now LaKiesha is vowing to break her family's cycle of drug use.

"I'm going to educate my children about drugs and the harm it can cause. I'm going to say, 'I don't want you to go down that road,'" LaKiesha says.

"It's a family history that I want to break."

CHAPTER 3

REDUCING AND PREVENTING TEEN ADDICTION

NEW MEASURES TO HELP TEENS QUIT SMOKING

Shari Roan

Researchers have long believed that teens who smoke do not want to quit, according to Shari Roan; recently, however, experts have discovered that many teens do want to quit but have a harder time doing so than adults. Smoking cessation programs designed to help adults quit smoking do not work as well for teens, the author writes, because teens need different kinds of intervention and support to keep them from returning to their nicotine habit. For instance, she explains, teen smokers have unique emotional and social issues linked to cigarette use, and they need to have a supportive school and home environment in order for their efforts at quitting to be successful. Many new programs are being implemented to help teens quit smoking, Roan reports, and some are showing early signs of success. Roan is the health writer for the *Los Angeles Times*.

Dr. Richard Hurt didn't hold out much hope the day he launched a drive to recruit volunteers for a Mayo Clinic study on smoking.

Hurt was looking for teenagers.

Teenagers who wanted to quit smoking.

Teens who would have to have parental consent, visit a clinic weekly and wear a nicotine patch for six weeks.

So Hurt was pleasantly surprised when more than 100 volunteers—13- to 17-year-olds who smoked at least 10 cigarettes a day—signed up. There were so many volunteers that he had to turn away dozens.

"There is a mythology out there that teen smokers don't want to stop," says Hurt, of the Mayo Clinic's Nicotine Dependence Center in Rochester, Minn. "That is not true. We just don't know how to help them very well."

But a burgeoning movement focused on efforts to stop teenagers from smoking is gaining momentum in this country, targeting a group of smokers who have been largely ignored for years.

Focusing Research on Teen Smokers

"It's been a very strange area of research," says Steve Sussman, an associate professor of preventive medicine at the University of Southern California (USC) and an authority on youth smoking cessation. "Back in 1982, the surgeon general report encouraged teen cessation. But there also has been kind of a folk wisdom among lay people and researchers that teens won't quit smoking, so you need to wait until they're young adults."

In 1999, the U.S. Centers for Disease Control and Prevention organized a conference on teen smoking cessation that amounted to "a call to begin doing research in this area," he says.

Efforts to help teenage smokers quit are also a response to a series of revelations about tobacco use, experts say. These insights include:

- Most smokers start as teens.
- The younger people start to smoke, the harder it is to quit.
- Health problems resulting from smoking begin to accrue quickly in young smokers.

Aimee Garten was a poster child for youth smoking. Garten, of Julian, California, began smoking at 12. By the time she entered USC in 1999, she was a two-pack-a-day smoker.

"When I started smoking, it was the cool thing to do," Garten says. Cigarettes were "easy to get and fairly cheap. Most of the people in liquor stores would sell to us without hassling us."

Many of those conditions have changed, thanks to a major California anti-tobacco initiative that began with passage of the Proposition 99 cigarette tax in 1988. Proposition 10, which took effect in 1999, boosted the tax on cigarettes by 50 cents a pack.

That caught Garten's attention.

"I sat down and calculated it," she says, "and realized I was spending $50 a month on cigarettes. When you're in college, money becomes a major issue.

"I also realized my health was being affected. I had asthma as a child, and it started up again. I was coughing up disgusting things every morning."

After several unsuccessful efforts to quit and four months of trying to simply cut back on the number of cigarettes she smoked daily, she was able to quit. Her asthma symptoms have eased dramatically.

"I have an elderly relative who is sick and refuses to quit smoking," Garten says. "I'm glad I'm not going to be like that."

Teens Do Try to Quit—Often

Garten isn't exceptional in her desire to quit. A landmark 1992 study from the University of Massachusetts Medical Center in Worcester found that 52% of 10th-grade smokers had already tried to quit two or more times.

The study also found that one-quarter of the teens thought they were addicted. And nearly half were concerned about their health.

While many teenagers apparently want to quit, they have an especially difficult time doing so. The few teen smoking cessation programs that have been scientifically evaluated show poor results.

Hurt's work is a case in point. In his recent study, published in January 2000 in the *Archives of Pediatric & Adolescent Medicine*, only 11 of 101 smokers had stopped at the end of six-week patch therapy. Six months later, only five remained abstinent.

He attributes the poor results to the fact that the patch study did not include much behavior intervention, which teaches things like what to do when a craving strikes. But others note that such intervention programs have fared poorly among adolescents.

Sussman examined 17 teen cessation programs using behavioral approaches (not including nicotine aids, like the patch) and found an average quit rate of 6% to 7%. In programs where kids seemed highly motivated, the quit rate was closer to 10%.

The typical adult quit rate after a cessation program is 50%.

"I think one of the problems with the programs developed early on is they were based on an adult model of cessation," Sussman says.

Teens Need a Different Approach

Research shows that in some ways, teen smokers are similar to their adult counterparts: They tend to smoke out of addiction or habit, to fit in socially, or to improve mood or relieve stress. According to a federal government study, most kids who smoke daily do so within two years of first trying a cigarette.

But kids differ on how they are persuaded to stop using nicotine.

"If you want kids to go to a clinic, you need to round them up," Sussman says. "If you want to keep them, you have to make it kind of fun. These are the things people hadn't been doing."

Most teen smoking cessation programs are funded through the state or county and are offered at high schools. Some are voluntary classes, while others target students who are caught smoking. These students are punished with a suspension, a fine or community service, Sussman says. Community service can include a cessation program.

Schools need to deal with student smokers in a helpful manner, Sussman says.

"While smoking is illegal, if a teen wants to quit, there needs to be a lot of support at that point," he says.

Support may be the most vital component of teen programs. Like adult smokers, adolescents experience withdrawal symptoms. But adolescents appear less able or willing to put up with the irritability, headaches or fatigue, and need more moral support during this phase.

"These kids need support," says Rita Moncrief, a teacher who oversees smoking cessation programs at El Camino Real High School in Woodland Hills, California. Moncrief keeps a supply of chewing gum and plastic straws in her classroom for ex-smokers to gnaw on if a craving strikes.

"It's amazing—their addiction. They find it very hard to quit. You would think that these are young kids and they haven't been smoking that long. But many have. I had one girl start when she was 8."

For teen girls, who often begin smoking as a way to control their weight, quitting poses the additional problem of weight gain.

Quitting can also be hampered if teens use other addictive substances, says Dr. Gary Wong, a preventive medicine expert at Kaiser Permanente Medical Center in Fontana, California.

"It's been shown that some adolescents start smoking and move to the illegal drugs," Wong says. For these kids, he says, therapy should address all addictive behavior.

Smoking and Socializing Go Together

Helping adolescents deal with the people around them who smoke— family and friends—is also a huge issue, Hurt says. Surveys show that 30% of adult smokers have another smoker at home. But among teen smokers, 75% have another smoker in the home. The presence of another smoker often deters those trying to quit.

"We asked the kids in our study if there was someone at home to help you, what would you want them to do?" Hurt says. "They said things like: Tell them not to smoke around me. Not to offer me cigarettes. Not to buy me cigarettes.

"The environmental factor is not a trivial one. As many teens wanted to bring a person in their household who is smoking into the study as wanted to stop smoking themselves."

Perhaps especially for teenagers, the social aspect of smoking complicates quitting. Garten, who met many of her college friends in areas where smokers congregate, found she had to drop those friends in order to quit.

"The reason I failed initially was because all my friends smoked," she said. "Finally my best friend decided to quit too, and he was really good at it. He really encouraged me. I'm not really friends with the smokers anymore."

James Chanthapak, a senior at Marshall High School in Los Angeles, tried to quit smoking in November 1999 on the American Cancer Society's Great American Smokeout Day. During the last few years, the cancer group has stepped up its campaign to target teens during the Smokeout with a "Teens Kick Ash" motto. Chanthapak was enthusiastic enough to quit for two or three weeks. But he couldn't sustain the effort.

"It's such a social thing," he says. "I would have had to change friends. Smoking is just what we do."

In the meantime, his habit has grown from one pack a week to three packs.

"I used to tell people that if you wanted to quit smoking, you could quit," he says, softly. "Now I think you need help. I didn't know it was as hard as it is."

Establishing Programs for Teens

Should Chanthapak decide to try to quit again, there are a range of options. And within the next year, cessation experts will have a better idea of what works with kids, Sussman says.

The enthusiasm to help teens is so great that some experts worry that programs may be implemented before they've been shown to work.

"People are trying the Internet, CD-ROMs, school programs, patches, all kinds of ways to approach the topic," Sussman says. "But there is a push toward getting programs out there quickly, before they are evaluated."

Sussman hopes to publish results soon from his program at a continuation high school that shows a quit rate of 17%, compared with 10% in a similar group that received no services.

At the University of California, San Diego, the results of a telephone counseling study involving 1,400 adolescents—which program directors say will be favorable—will be released in May 2000. In that program, teens who call in are assigned a telephone counselor who regularly contacts them.

Studies will also continue on nicotine aids, like the patch, gum or the antidepressant medication Zyban. Those aids shouldn't be ruled out for teens despite poor early results, Hurt says. Although few kids in his study quit smoking, the teens cooperated with wearing the patch and many dramatically cut back on the number of cigarettes they smoked.

And then there was that most hopeful sign: They wanted to quit.

"When we got the final results, we said, 'Oh, no,'" says Hurt. "But when we started peeling away the layers, there are some positive things happening."

Enlisting Teens in the Fight Against Tobacco

Patricia Sosa

Patricia Sosa is the director of constituency relations for the Campaign for Tobacco-Free Kids, an anti-smoking organization located in Washington, D.C. In the following article, Sosa discusses the efforts of young people from around the country to reduce and prevent tobacco use among their peers. These teens take part in a variety of anti-tobacco activities, she explains, such as organizing marches and rallies, testifying before their elected officials, and helping to author legislation designed to limit youths' access to tobacco products. According to the author, teens are a powerful force in the fight against tobacco and should be encouraged to join the adults in this campaign. Sosa hopes that community advocacy, coupled with comprehensive tobacco legislation, will lead to a victory in the war against youth tobacco use.

The year 1998 has been an historic time in the fight against Big Tobacco. But 1999 holds the promise of making even greater strides in the effort to keep US children tobacco-free.

In 1997, several provisions of the Food and Drug Administration (FDA) rule regulating tobacco as a drug began to take effect, including toughening enforcement of laws prohibiting the sale of tobacco products to minors. Big Tobacco predictably balked, taking the federal government to court to preserve its right to continue marketing to kids.

No sooner had the FDA won a partial victory against the tobacco industry in a federal court in Greensboro, North Carolina, than the historic settlement was reached between 40 state attorneys general and the nation's largest tobacco companies. Those companies had been sued by the states to recoup the cost of caring for thousands of Medicaid patients sick or dying from tobacco-related illness.

The settlement set in force the momentum for drafting the toughest tobacco control legislation in history. It would, among other things, further restrict the marketing of tobacco products to children, establish financial penalties for the industry if youth tobacco use is

Reprinted, with permission, from "Kids Kicking Butts," by Patricia Sosa, *Christian Social Action*, June 1998.

not reduced, and grant full authority to the FDA to regulate tobacco products in much the same way the agency regulates other drugs.

What form a final bill will take remains to be seen. However, as Congress continues to debate the merits of Sen. John McCain's (R-AZ) bill and others, the battle to protect our nation's children from the lure of tobacco rages on in large and small ways all across the country.

Big Tobacco's Enemy

Increasingly, that battle is being fought by the very group that has been most seriously harmed by the tobacco companies in the past and that stands to lose the most in the future. Kids are Big Tobacco's number one target—and they are quickly becoming its number one enemy.

The past few years have seen a dramatic surge in youth advocacy, as kids all over America have come to realize that they are not merely victims and not merely part of the problem. They can also be a powerful part of the solution, and many of them are.

Consider, for example, the tremendous rise in participation in Kick Butts Day, the annual opportunity for US kids to engage in activities that put the tobacco companies on notice that they will no longer tolerate being lured into smoking through slick advertising campaigns and giveaways. Sponsored jointly by the Campaign for Tobacco-Free Kids and New York City Public Advocate Mark Green, this once-yearly national youth activists' day spiked to a record 400-plus events in April, 1998, up from 82 events in 1997.

All over America, young people organized rallies on their state capitol steps, lobbied for increases in tobacco excise taxes, pushed for local ordinances to ban cigarette vending machines, applied pressure to restaurants to prohibit smoking for diners, and conducted mock funerals and trials for Mr. Butts in a show of protest for the way the tobacco industry has profited at the expense of their health.

"In 1997, America's kids showed they have a powerful voice in the fight against tobacco," said campaign President Bill Novelli. "This year, that voice has grown even louder."

These young people were not alone. While they took the initiative, planned the events and came up with creative new ways to strike back against the industry, they were joined in cities and towns across the country by adult community activists, local elected officials, state attorneys general, congressmen and senators, and representatives from 17 federal agencies. No less than six Cabinet members and Vice President Al Gore all took part in Kick Butts Day activities around the nation to let US children know that the country's adults were standing behind them.

This is just one way that this country's young people are joining the front lines of this crucial public health battle.

Numerous teens spend their free time year-round devising new ways to counter the tobacco industry's powerful influence on their peers. Every year, the campaign recognizes the country's top young tobacco control activists with the Youth Advocates of the Year Awards, a national honor bestowed during a gala celebration in Washington, D.C., and attended by the movers and shakers of the tobacco control movement.

Anna Markee, the campaign's 1997 National Youth Advocate of the Year, explained what motivates her and other young people to commit to this cause. "For decades, the tobacco industry has been profiting at our expense," she said. "But now we are fighting back. Eventually, they'll learn that our lungs are not for sale."

On April 30, 1998, the campaign recognized five regional Youth Advocates, a national winner and the first-ever group winner as 1998 Youth Advocates of the Year. These young activists will continue to work with the campaign throughout the coming year to push for comprehensive national tobacco control legislation and other policy changes that can save kids' lives.

Here are just a few of the achievements cited by the campaign when recognizing 1998's winners:

• Emily Broxterman, 16, of Overland Park, Kansas, each year helps to organize an annual march and rally at her state capitol to mobilize young people from all across Kansas to push for tougher tobacco control laws. She works with local merchants to encourage them to make it tougher for minors to purchase tobacco products, testifies before the state legislature and travels to local schools speaking to younger students about the harmful effects of tobacco use. Emily is the campaign's 1998 National Youth Advocate of the Year.

• Michael Higgins, 13, of Monroeville, New Jersey, helped to draft and push through a local ordinance banning vending machines in his home township. The ordinance was then used as a model by other towns in his county. His current goal is to pass a county-wide ban. Michael is the campaign's 1998 East Regional Youth Advocate of the Year.

• Deanna Durrett, 16, of Louisville, Kentucky, testified before the Kentucky House of Representatives, urging its members to adopt tougher tobacco control policies statewide. To help her peers learn how to contact their legislators and how to lobby for tougher laws to reduce teen smoking, she organized a rally on her state capitol steps. Two hundred of her fellow teens showed up. Deanna is the campaign's 1998 South Regional Youth Advocate of the Year.

• Gretchen Sneegas, 11, of Indianapolis, Indiana, organized a protest outside her state capitol building after the state legislature overrode former Governor Evan Bayh's veto of legislation that took away the right of local governments to restrict the sale of tobacco products to minors. Later, she took up the charge for a statewide ban on cigarette vending machines. Gretchen is the campaign's 1998 Midwest Region Youth Advocate of the Year.

• Amanda Tunnell, 16, of Oklahoma City, Oklahoma, testified in support of a bill that allows Oklahoma cities to license tobacco retailers and fine those caught selling tobacco products to minors. Her concern about second-hand smoke and how it affects people like her mother, who has asthma, inspired her to survey local restaurants and encourage more of them to provide a smoke-free environment for customers. Amanda is the campaign's 1998 Central Region Youth Advocate of the Year.

• Annie Aguilar, 17, of Alhambra, California, spoke before Members of Congress about the prevalence of tobacco ads to which kids are subjected on a daily basis and created a guidebook and video to teach other kids how to become tobacco control advocates. Annie is the campaign's 1998 West Regional Youth Advocate of the Year.

• The S.H.O.C.K. Coalition (Saving the Health of Our Communities and Kids), a group of close to 40 teens from Brooklyn, New York, collected 4,200 signatures and 3,000 letters in support of the Youth Protection Against Tobacco Advertising and Promotion Act, which made it illegal to place tobacco advertising within 1,000 feet of any school, playground or child care facility in the five boroughs of New York City. The S.H.O.C.K. Coalition is the campaign's first-ever winner of the Group Youth Advocates of the Year Award.

"These young people have accomplished a great deal," Novelli said. "Their outstanding efforts to motivate their peers, mobilize legislators and protect new generations from tobacco addiction are truly remarkable."

Expanding Youth Advocacy Outreach

In addition to the Youth Advocates of the Year Awards, the campaign has begun several other initiatives to encourage involvement from kids and communities in the fight for a smoke-free environment for children. This year, the campaign is expanding its youth advocacy outreach by working in partnership with the Public Relations Society of America (PRSA) in 12 pilot projects across the country. PRSA members are paired with young people anxious to learn the tools of advocacy and public relations, and these highly motivated professionals are working with them to teach them those tools.

The campaign also offers opportunities to adults who want to join the "tobacco wars." It created a National Action Network of 12,000 activists from across the country. These crucial "field workers" are called upon to write letters to their congressmen and senators supporting critical legislation and to take an active role in pushing for initiatives that will help reduce teen smoking.

At any given time, there are countless other tobacco control efforts taking place all across the nation, sponsored by campaign partners, such as the American Heart Association, American Cancer Society and others. Still, much remains to be done.

Never before has the need for involvement been so great. Despite all of these efforts, by thousands of committed activists, smoking among high school seniors as of 1998 has reached a 19-year high; more than one in three seniors smokes. Every day, 6,000 teenagers pick up a cigarette for the first time, and 3,000 of them become regular, daily smokers. A third of those new smokers will die prematurely from tobacco-related disease.

Sadly, the average kid begins smoking at age 13, meaning many start much earlier. Children are taking their first tentative puffs on a cigarette before they graduate from elementary school.

These figures may seem daunting, but 1998 holds the best opportunity yet to reduce substantially teen smoking and start driving those numbers down.

Tobacco Control Legislation

Senator McCain and others in Congress have introduced comprehensive tobacco control legislation for the first time in this nation's history. Public health advocates are urging Congress to pass a strong, national tobacco control plan now—not several years from now.

"Each day that we delay is paid for with our children's health," said campaign President Novelli.

ENACT, a coalition of public health groups—including the Campaign for Tobacco-Free Kids—has organized in support of swift passage of a national tobacco control plan. The group is calling for a national policy that would include an increase in the price of cigarettes of at least $1.50 per pack; tough penalties for the tobacco industry if youth-smoking reduction goals are not met; strong protections against second-hand smoke; full authority for the Food and Drug Administration to regulate tobacco; adequate funding for public education, research, smoking cessation and other anti-tobacco programs; restrictions on tobacco marketing to children; and further restrictions on youth access to tobacco products.

However, there is always room—and the need—for more people to join in this historic push for a long-term solution to the country's growing pediatric epidemic of tobacco addiction.

In addition to encouraging Members of Congress to pass comprehensive tobacco legislation, those who want to join this battle can also take a page from the youth advocates' play book. They can organize local tobacco control activities such as rallies, protests and marches; speak to local school children about the dangers of tobacco use; lobby for bans on tobacco billboard ads near schools; or join the campaign's National Action Network.

"Today, a window of opportunity exists to save millions of lives," Novelli said. "We need to act now, before it closes. Let's follow the lead of young activists all across America and begin fighting back. A victory in this 'war' is a victory your children will thank you for."

LAW ENFORCEMENT STRATEGIES FOR REDUCING UNDERAGE DRINKING

Bobby Little and Mike Bishop

Law enforcement personnel often do not make it a priority to enforce laws that are intended to keep teens from obtaining and consuming alcohol, Bobby Little and Mike Bishop relate in the following article. However, they point out, alcohol consumption by minors can be dangerous and can lead to addiction. Little and Bishop offer a variety of strategies that law enforcement agencies can use to combat this important problem, including undercover stings at establishments where alcohol is sold to teens. The authors also suggest legislative solutions aimed at curbing underage access to alcohol and reducing the likelihood of alcohol-related accidents, deaths, and injuries involving minors. Little is a professor of criminal justice at High Point University in North Carolina. Bishop is the district supervisor for the Alabama Alcoholic Beverage Control Enforcement Division in Florence, Alabama.

Several sophisticated criminological research projects have confirmed empirically something that law enforcement practitioners have known for a long time: many officers simply do not make teenage alcohol use an enforcement priority. One study surveyed a sample of police personnel and found that many officers rate this type of enforcement activity among the lowest of police responsibilities. A second study revealed that some of the reasons police offered for assigning a low priority to this type of crime included perceived legal obstacles associated with processing juveniles and the unpleasant paperwork and special detention procedures required for minors. Officers also cited such reasons as a lack of juvenile detention facilities or inadequate space inside existing centers, the lack of significant punishment for teen alcohol use, and disagreement with some of the laws regulating underage drinking, especially the illegality of alcohol consumption by adults ages 18 through 20. Although some of these objections represent legitimate concerns, many valid reasons exist for making enforcement of underage alcohol use a higher priority. A factually based rationale for making alcohol violations a priority combined with

Reprinted from "Minor Drinkers/Major Consequences: Enforcement Strategies for Underage Alcoholic Beverage Law Violators," by Bobby Little and Mike Bishop, *FBI Law Enforcement Bulletin*, June 1998. Endnotes in the original have been omitted in this reprint.

proven strategies for deterring the illegal purchase, possession, and consumption of alcohol by minors stands the best chance of addressing this growing concern.

The Factual Rationale

Most adults remember taking their first drink at a young age; for some, getting drunk was a rite of passage. To these individuals, underage drinking is a harmless activity, a victimless crime. Yet, the fact remains: underage drinking can have devastating consequences and demands serious attention.

More teens die in alcohol-related motor vehicle crashes than from any other cause. Alcohol use also contributes to a significant proportion of other types of teenage deaths, such as drownings, suicides, and recreational fatalities. Teenage alcoholism is alarmingly high in the United States and is associated with crimes ranging from petty larceny to homicide. The economic losses alone from alcohol-related property damage, lost productivity, and other detrimental consequences associated with alcohol abuse cost society tens of billions of dollars per year.

In addition to the death toll, property damage, and economic losses, tens of thousands of people are injured seriously in alcohol-related mishaps every year. These accidents occur on the job, around the home, and during social activities.

Medical studies have documented the detrimental effects of alcohol on the human liver, stomach, pancreas, and other internal organs. Chronic alcohol abuse can lead to alcoholism, exacerbating the toll on the body. Young female alcoholics put their unborn children at risk for fetal alcohol syndrome.

Finally, the public wants the police to address the problem of underage drinking. In many states, legislatures have passed or are considering passing tougher laws associated with both adult drunk driving and alcohol use by minors. Examples include raising the legal drinking age, lowering the blood-alcohol content (BAC) for legally defined levels of intoxication, enacting stiffer penalties for drunk driving, suspending the driver's licenses of youths caught purchasing or possessing alcohol, and prohibiting licensed, juvenile drivers from operating motor vehicles during certain hours, such as midnight to 5 A.M.

In short, the loss of life, property damage, economic costs, and negative health effects associated with underage drinking, as well as public outcry for police attention, provide sufficient reasons to make the illegal use of alcohol by teens a greater concern among police agencies. To do so, law enforcement agencies can employ a number of tactics.

Undercover Stings

About 90 percent of high school students have tried alcohol, and approximately 60 percent of both high school and college students drink regularly. Forty percent of college students regularly "binge-drink," defined as consuming five or more drinks consecutively; 4 percent of students drink every day.

Unfortunately, the ease with which underage drinkers can purchase alcohol represents a national problem. In an effort to combat this problem, many police agencies supplement surveillance activities with sting operations, during which a minor operative attempts to purchase alcohol from various licensed establishments, such as convenience stores, restaurants, and bars.

Agencies need to take precautions prior to such operations. The commander of the agency should interview and assess the suitability of minors prior to approving their use for paid employment or volunteer work. In some states, additional legal guidelines apply. In Alabama, for example, the minor's parent or guardian must sign a consent form and provide the law enforcement agency with a copy of the child's birth certificate, driver's license, and a recent photograph. In addition, agency policies may require that personnel conducting a sting provide a supervisor with a proposed operational plan for approval prior to action. Further, the attempted purchase should be audio- or videotaped, and money used in the operation should be marked and retrieved whenever possible. When the operative is used in an on-premise location, such as a restaurant, lounge, or club, an undercover officer or agent should take a position inside the establishment to observe the potential sale.

All law enforcement agencies using minor operatives should consider adopting such guidelines as standard operating procedure. Still, officers should contact the local prosecutor or judicial authority before using an operative. In some states, using minors as operatives may present the potential for legal challenge by the defense counsel or may not be legal at all.

Despite the inherent difficulties in using a minor operative, such sting operations have met with success. When Alabama Alcoholic Beverage Control (ABC) officers initiated this technique, approximately 70 percent of the establishments sold alcohol to the underage operative. Following several years of making cases using this technique, the proportion of establishments selling to minor operatives dropped to about 25 percent.

Cops 'N Shops

The Cops 'N Shops program is popular with alcohol merchants in many states, and it produces some deterrent effect on youths trying to purchase alcoholic beverages. The purpose of the program is threefold: to curb the purchase of alcoholic beverages by minors, to assist retail licensees in their efforts to operate their establishments within legal guidelines, and to lower the number of minors who drink and drive. Cops 'N Shops differs from undercover stings in that it focuses on the violator, rather than the alcoholic beverage retail industry.

Individuals of legal drinking age who purchase alcohol to sell or give to minors represent a secondary target for this type of operation.

Traditionally, an agent or officer poses as an employee or a customer in a retail establishment, waiting to arrest any minor attempting to purchase alcohol. Sometimes, illegal transactions take place in the parking lot between individuals who legally purchase the alcohol to give to minors waiting outside. Placing a backup officer outside nets these offenders.

Attempts to deter unlawful buyers include special signs to scare those contemplating the offense. These Cops 'N Shops signs, placed at all entrances, notify everyone entering the store that agents may pose as employees and warn that any person violating the law will be prosecuted. Though retailers are sometimes reluctant to participate in the program, Cops 'N Shops has become a viable enforcement strategy in many states.

Party Patrols

Another enforcement strategy involves the use of party patrols. These patrols appear to be the easiest way to make a large number of arrests for underage drinking. Typically, informants at local high schools and universities tip off law enforcement to underage drinkers planning a party. Undercover operatives can attend such gatherings, or officers acting alone can surveil the location and make arrests. A weekend drunk driving and party patrol program in Oregon increased the arrest of minors for possession from 60 to 1,000 in 1 year. There also was a corresponding decrease of 35 percent in underage and young adult automobile crashes. When not hunting teenage parties and citing underage drinkers, the officers operated sobriety checkpoints and conducted drunk driving enforcement patrols.

Walk-Throughs

The walk-through is a method of observing activity inside alcoholic beverage retail outlets such as bars and restaurants. Officers may enter such public places either covertly, in plain clothes, or overtly, in uniform. The obvious advantage of covert entry is that it lets the officer observe alcohol violations without evoking the suspicion of customers or employees. This technique enables officers to spot violations by customers, including attempts to illegally purchase or consume alcoholic beverages or to provide alcohol to underage drinkers. Walk-throughs also allow officers to scrutinize bartenders and other employees who may be serving underage patrons.

In Alabama, the alcoholic beverage industry is considered heavily regulated, and as a result, law enforcement officers with proper jurisdiction may conduct administrative searches or inspections of licensed premises without search warrants. The law in other states may not condone an intensive search without a warrant, but it may allow a walk-through to look for violations. Officers should check with their local prosecutors before employing these techniques.

Legislative Action

Certain legislative and policy actions may effectively deter teenage alcohol use and reduce the number of alcohol-related crashes among young drivers. Many states have lowered the legally acceptable levels of blood-alcohol content for drivers under 21. In Alabama, for example, a youth under age 21 caught operating a motor vehicle with .02 BAC or above is charged with driving under the influence. Two other legislative proposals include laws prohibiting driving by young, novice drivers between certain times, especially midnight to 5 A.M., and a 90-day license suspension for youths convicted of possessing alcoholic beverages or using a false driver's license to purchase alcohol.

Simply put, underage drinking is against the law. Yet, in a culture that views alcohol consumption as a part of growing up, even those tasked with enforcing the law may overlook violations. The many consequences of irresponsible drinking, by youths and adults alike, demand action.

During a time of increasing attention to other drugs of abuse, such as marijuana and cocaine, police administrators who must operate with limited financial resources may have difficulty allocating the necessary staff to combat the underage drinking problem. Yet, with help from policy makers, retailers, and the public, agencies can implement innovative enforcement strategies to curb underage drinking.

PERSUADING YOUTHS THAT HOPS AIN'T HIP

Mike Mitka

In the following selection, Mike Mitka discusses new research concerning ways to reduce and prevent binge drinking by young Americans. In particular, he examines the results of a study focusing on California teens who regularly cross the border to Mexico—where the legal drinking age is only eighteen—in order to drink and party. The study aims to curb this behavior by exploring the reasons it occurs in the first place, Mitka explains; this information will ultimately be used to help prevent binge drinking among youths throughout the United States. Mitka also describes the efforts at several U.S. universities to find and institute community-based solutions to the problem of binge drinking. Mitka is an associate editor for the *Journal of the American Medical Association* (*JAMA*).

As some hip-hopping young Americans help pack the Safari Club on Tijuana's Avenida Revolución chugging beers, guzzling tequila, and "Gittin' Jiggy Wit' It," one can understand if they forget they're helping advance medical research. But they are.

Before entering Mexico, at the border crossing on the California side, young men and women under the age of 21 are randomly selected and asked about their motives and expectations for visiting Tijuana. They face more questions upon their return. Their answers and blood-alcohol levels are anonymously recorded as part of an ongoing study by researchers from the Pacific Institute for Research and Evaluation who hope to provide some data on why young people binge drink. The information is passed along to those hoping to curb such drinking patterns.

Reducing Binge Drinking

Binge drinking (defined as 5 or more alcoholic drinks in a row for men and 4 or more for women by researchers with the Harvard School of Public Health) among young adults leads to impairment that can result in drunk driving, sexual assault, violence, and a host of other adverse effects. The Pacific Institute researchers, who are working in collaboration with the San Diego, Calif–based Institute for Health Advocacy (IHA), are trying to document the characteristics and motivations of young Americans binge drinking in Tijuana. At the same time, they are trying to reduce the numbers of binge drinkers and the severity of their alcohol consumption. They hope their efforts are successful and can be replicated throughout the United States.

"Our major goal is to track change," said James E. Lange, PhD, a research psychologist with the Bethesda, Md–based Pacific Institute and coauthor of a paper—presented in May 1998 at the Alcohol Policy Conference XI in Chicago, Ill—documenting initial research results from the border-crossing effort. "But another important component is to provide information to those trying to effect change so they can use that information to tailor their programs and get results."

The border isn't the only place where researchers are trying to reduce binge drinking in young adults. The Robert Wood Johnson Foundation (RWJ) is funding a multiyear, $10-million national program called "A Matter of Degree: Reducing High-Risk Drinking Among College Students." Administered by the American Medical Association (AMA), the program forms college-community partnerships designed to change the environment and norms regarding high-risk drinking by students. Six sites are currently funded: the University of Colorado at Boulder, University of Delaware, University of Iowa, Lehigh University, University of Vermont, and University of Wisconsin at Madison. Two other colleges are in the process of joining the program.

The RWJ effort doesn't focus on why students binge drink. These program leaders want only to reduce the number of binge drinkers and the secondhand damage associated with such high-risk behavior. Lange wants to know why these people drink the way they do. He said such information should help in designing prevention or reduced-drinking programs.

Lange's preliminary results, from the first few months of a 4-year study, found that the motivation to drink is partly attributable to expectations about the effects of alcohol. Those interviewed before entering Mexico answer a word-association question. Young adults who associated "drunk" with the words, "fight, hurt, and knife," expected to drink less than those who associated "drunk" with "fun, friends, and kiss." And upon their return those with negative associations did drink less than those with positive ones. Another point made by Lange is that drinking isn't the only reason young adults go to Tijuana—they also go to meet people, blow off steam, and "go a little crazy." Lange called this "social scene motivation." He noted that those who associated drinking with positive words also planned to get drunk as part of the social scene motivation. Interestingly, those who associated drinking with negative words sought the same social scene motivation without planning to get drunk.

"We may know this, but it hasn't been quantified—people are going down there to drink and get drunk. It's not just social pressure or refusal skills that we must focus on when trying to curb binge drinking," Lange said. "That's something we need to keep in mind when we think about alcohol abuse and substance abuse in general—it's not just learning to say no, it's learning how not to say yes."

Learning Not to Say Yes

Jeffrey D. Francis, deputy program director with IHA, is trying to get young drinkers not to say yes. On a tour of Tijuana, Francis commented on some of Avenida Revolución's 35 discos or bars. He noted the all-you-can-drink-for-$5 specials and the women-drink-free opportunities and showed a postcard mailed to Californians on their 18th birthday touting the Tijuana scene as their local bar.

To combat the aggressive tactics of Tijuana bar owners, antibinge leaders are using several approaches. One is an increased police presence on the California side, where officers periodically check IDs and administer Breathalyzer tests on such "celebratory" occasions as Labor Day weekend or during spring break. Another, said Dana Stevens, IHA's youth services manager, is to work with area colleges and military bases to make them aware that their students and enlisted people, not identified by name, are going to Tijuana, getting drunk, and driving back. "We've been able to define this problem and put the word out clearly," she said.

Yet a third approach is working with leaders on the Mexican side. These officials know that Tijuana's growing reputation as a binge-drinking party town is affecting tourism by keeping older, and more affluent, Americans away, said Saul Cana, IHA's international coordination manager. "We try to focus this as a Mexican solution," said Cana, who recently became a US citizen but still practices law in Mexico. "We're trying to let them know we're supporting their efforts and we're trying to help them with this program. We're not doing anything they'd not do. This isn't gringos trying to take over Baja." Some of the Mexican efforts include stricter ID checks, toning down the marketing, and consideration of raising the drinking age to 21.

Curbing Binge Drinking on Campus

While the Pacific Institute and IHA continue their border research and initiatives, the RWJ program is tracking the problem on college campuses. Richard Yoast, PhD, the AMA's director of the Office of Alcohol and Other Drug Abuse, said the "Matter of Degree" program language is simple: "We want to change the community in which drinking occurs to make it harder to binge drink." The program focuses on 3 main elements: lessening availability; increasing price (low prices up consumption); and changing norms.

At the University of Wisconsin, a 21-member partnership council made up of students, faculty, and community leaders is overseeing 3 task forces addressing campus policies and practices, media and education, and community policies and practices. The school's Rob Adsit, coordinator of the RWJ project, said some of the plans include offering recreational sports after 10 PM on Fridays and Saturdays to give students a social option other than drinking. Another effort includes working with some community members to open a dance club with a large nonalcohol section.

Rick Culliton, assistant to the vice president for student affairs at the University of Vermont, said actions his school is taking include elimination of alcohol advertising from the athletic department's media guides and changing the school year to avoid opening around Labor Day and giving a 3-day weekend for drinking. They want students to have 5 full days of classes at the beginning of the semester. "We're sending a message that a student's academic experience will be rigorous," he said.

The University of Iowa is creating an alcohol-free parking lot outside the football stadium for the first home game so people can have tailgate parties and stay sober, said Julie Phye, coordinator of the Stepping-Up Project. The students are also getting into the act. The fraternities and sororities were supposed to go dry by 1999, but the members, wanting to take a stance against alcohol abuse, moved the deadline up to the fall of 1998.

A COMPREHENSIVE STRATEGY FOR PREVENTING TEEN HEROIN ABUSE

Donna Shalala

The following selection is taken from a September 29, 1997, speech by Donna Shalala, then the U.S. Secretary of Health and Human Services, at a conference of the National Institute on Drug Abuse. Shalala notes that while drug abuse among teens has declined overall in recent years, the popularity of heroin has skyrocketed. The heroin problem among teens can best be addressed through a comprehensive strategy that combines strict law enforcement, treatment programs, and research to find more effective treatments for heroin addiction, she maintains. Also important, Shalala continues, are measures designed to combat the glamorous image of heroin as portrayed in fashion and popular culture. However, she concludes, the most crucial measure may be for parents, teachers, and the community to send early, consistent, and repeated messages to children and teens about the dangers of using heroin. Shalala is currently the president of the University of Miami.

I was thinking about this conference the other day when I drove past Union Station. It said that [U.S. Supreme Court] Justice Oliver Wendell Holmes once boarded a train there, and in the general confusion, he lost his ticket. The conductor immediately recognized Oliver Wendell Holmes and said, "Never mind, Mr. Justice. When you find your ticket, I'm certain that you'll mail it in."

"Mr. Conductor," replied the justice, "the question isn't where is my ticket, but where am I supposed to be going."

I tell this story because in our journey to end the tragedy of heroin addiction, there are no one-way tickets and there are no express routes. But scientific research can tell us where we are, and it can guide us to where we need to go.

Fighting a Battle Against Heroin

First, we know that research can lift the veil from the current face of heroin. And what we see is that although heroin continues to plague

Reprinted from Donna Shalala's speech delivered at the National Institute on Drug Abuse Conference on Heroin Use, Washington, DC, September 29, 1997.

all Americans, its trap is increasingly ensnaring our young people. Young people, like a young woman I heard about named Cathy. Our children are returning to school right now, but Cathy won't be going with them. She was only 17 years old; she was full of hope and promise, and waging a battle against her own drug addiction.

But like the ancient sirens whose singing lured mariners to their deaths, heroin's pull was too much for Cathy. One night she decided to go with two friends to buy heroin. It was cheap, it was easy to get, and this time it was deadly. This time Cathy had a bad reaction. She went into convulsions and momentarily stopped breathing, and the next morning her father found her dead.

Imagine how you would feel as a parent, your only child lost to heroin. Unfortunately, Cathy's father is not alone. Because of our work and the work of others, we have seen a glimmer of hope in the fight to keep our children away from drugs, but just a glimmer.

The 1996 household drug survey showed us that drug use among teens declined for the first time since 1992. And teen use of alcohol and marijuana has leveled off.

But despite the encouraging news, we can hardly claim victory—not when the same study showed for the first time heroin use by teenagers increased four-fold from the 1980s to 1995; not when the number of teenage girls admitted for heroin addiction to substance abuse centers that receive public funds increased by nearly 20 percent from 1992 into the middle of the 1990s; and not when there were more than 140,000 new heroin users in 1995. Most of the new heroin users were under 26. We can't let this trend continue.

We have to fight this battle for the child who is smoking heroin and letting a life of promise and potential go up in a puff of smoke. We must fight it for the adolescent who is buying drugs and mortgaging their future hopes and dreams, and we have to fight it for young girls like Cathy, so that they never share her fate. And we must fight this battle on every front, which is the second lesson that I think research teaches us.

Strategies to Combat Heroin

We need an anti-heroin strategy—indeed, an anti-drug strategy—that attacks the problem from every angle. That strategy is comprehensive, tough and bold. . . .

The strategy includes law enforcement. We want to send a clear message that everyone who sells heroin or any drug should be prosecuted, and so that we stop the cartels and their street-level dealers long before they can seduce our kids with their poison.

But the strategy must also include treatment and prevention. . . . Under Dr. [Alan] Leshner's leadership, the National Institute on Drug Abuse is doing cutting-edge research on the science of addiction and how heroin can actually change an addict's brain. This research will allow us to discover and formulate more effective treatments for heroin addiction, and that's important.

In a study of over 4,100 clients in federally funded substance abuse programs, it showed that a year after treatment the rate of respondents reporting heroin use declined 46 percent. And our Substance Abuse and Mental Health Services Administration is going to be listening to what comes out of this conference so we can study and implement some of the most promising new treatment approaches as part of our youth heroin initiative.

But we must also continue to prevent heroin abuse and all drug abuse before it starts, and we must do it in a targeted and a sophisticated way. Our research clearly shows that people start using drugs and keep using drugs for very different reasons, kids for different reasons than adults, and girls for different reasons than boys. Our strategy must reflect that.

And that's the purpose of the department's Girl Power campaign. We know that the gender gap in substance abuse has narrowed. We know that girls from nine to 14 face unique challenges and barriers, and we knew that we needed to create messages and programs for girls not only preventing drug abuse and other risky behaviors, but also giving them the confidence they need to get active, to get strong, and to make the most of their lives.

Research can continue to help us understand why young people are specifically using heroin, what motivates young girls and boys to start, what kinds of innovative strategies could we enlist to make sure that they never do. That is our challenge, and that must be our mandate.

Sending Anti-Drug Messages to Children

Which leads me to my third and my final point. I've talked a lot about teenagers today, partly because that's where most drug abuse starts in this country. But research has shown us that we can't wait until then to talk to our kids about drugs. If we want to immunize our children against the threat of heroin, we must find anti-drug messages that work, and we must send them early and often. Early and often.

Data from the Partnership for a Drug-Free America shows that children tend to have strong anti-drug attitudes right up until the age of 12. But those attitudes begin to change right before the teen years as kids start to receive an assault of pro-use messages from popular culture and other sources.

I recently went to an elementary school. [U.S. Drug Czar General] Barry [McCaffrey] and I often are directed by the White House, as they direct the Cabinet, to go off to schools, particularly at the beginning of the school year. And for those of us that don't think that public health messages get through to kids, I went to a class of first-graders. And as I was leaving after I'd read the kids a book and talked to them for a while, I asked them for messages for the president. They gave me three messages. Number one, tell him to wash his hands before he eats.

Number two, tell him to look both ways before he crosses the street. And number three, tell him not to smoke anything.

Kids get their attitudes early. It's keeping those attitudes. We have to speak as one voice, sustaining our children's initial anti-drug attitudes through their teen years so they never fall victim like Cathy to the seductive siren of pro-use messages or the fatal glamour of heroin.

Heroin Is Not Glamorous

Three times in this century, during its opening years at the height of the Jazz Age and throughout much of the 1960s and the 1970s, heroin was thought to be glamorous. Three times. Each time the glamour faded, usually because of the death of a celebrity.

But anyone who hoped that it was finally gone with the Age of Aquarius, buried with victims like Jimi Hendrix and Janis Joplin and Jim Morrison, were sadly mistaken. Only this time it's particularly stalking young girls.

Too often today when girls open a fashion magazine, instead of seeing pictures of health, they see pictures of heroin chic—models with drawn faces, eyes rimmed in black smudges, almost deathlike. Long before they enter adolescence, we need to send our kids anti-drug messages that will drown out the pro-use messages blaring from magazines and from music. We need to tell them that any style, song or show that glamorizes heroin use is mirroring the reality of addiction in a funhouse mirror.

And we need to convince them that heroin is not the stuff of dreams, but the stuff of nightmares. We have to deglamorize heroin once and for all in this country, so that no future generation is ever seduced by its deadly charms.

Reinforcing the Anti-Drug Message

The task may seem daunting, but we don't think it's impossible. When we as a nation focus on a problem, when we raise our voices, when we involve parents, when we involve teachers and community leaders in the fight, we can always make a difference. We need to keep up a steady drum beat of anti-drug messages echoing from every corner of this society.

Parents are the single most profound influence on our children. They need to sit down at the kitchen table and talk to their kids early and often. But their guidance has to be reinforced when the children leave the house. Coaches and clergy and teachers, the media and everyone else in our children's lives, need to tell them early and often that heroin chic is not attractive. It's ugly and it's deadly.

Scientists and researchers must find new ways to tell our kids early and often that heroin attacks the body, assaults the brain and assaults the spirit. And all of us need to tell them early and often that heroin kills. We must do it now.

I'm reminded that Oliver Wendell Holmes, perhaps even on that famous trip on the train, once noted, "The greatest thing in this world is not so much where we stand, as to what directions we're moving." I know that all of you will help us move forward in our battle against heroin, and I know that, working together, we're going to win.

Participation in Artistic Programs Can Reduce Teen Drug Addiction

Harvey Milkman

Harvey Milkman is a professor of psychology at Metropolitan State College in Denver, Colorado. He is also the director of Project Self Discovery, a program that encourages teens to participate in artistic alternatives to drug use. In the following article, Milkman explains that teens often turn to drugs to help them escape the boredom or pain of their everyday lives. The purpose of Project Self Discovery, Milkman writes, is to encourage teens to use art, music, and dance as a way to express themselves and cope with their problems without resorting to drugs. Artistic expression provides a viable alternative to drugs for teens who are looking to bring more happiness and stability into their lives, he maintains. In addition, nontraditional therapies such as Project Self Discovery can help at-risk teens identify new ways to deal with self-destructive behaviors and negative emotions, he concludes.

At home, his mother would ignore David and his sisters. She loved to drink with her men friends. When she let one of them move in, he would beat everyone up. Going to school was no better. He figured the only way to fit in was by using drugs and drinking. When he joined the Junior Reserves Officers Training Corps (JROTC), he found the common link was doing drugs. Because of his habits, he was failing his classes. During his sophomore year, he went to class a total of nine days. Soon enough, he just didn't go. He hated himself so much he even attempted suicide. He tried hanging himself and overdosing on aspirin.

At about that time he also started to eat a lot. In less than a year, he had gained over a hundred pounds. He was so alienated from his family that he barely spoke to his mom. Whenever she asked to talk he would tell her to go to hell. Then at the age of 16, David had a mild heart attack. Drugs were the reason behind his heart problems. Right then he decided to quit.

Reprinted from "Better than Dope," by Harvey Milkman, *Psychology Today,* March/April 2001. Copyright © 1999 by Sussex Publishers, Inc. Reprinted with permission from *Psychology Today.*

After that summer, he enrolled into school. His guidance counselor told David about our program, Project Self Discovery. PSD is a community-based afterschool program that provides artistic alternatives to teenagers who have problems with school, their families or the community. Participants use music, art and dance to reach their goals. David signed up for the music program. Although his story is unique, his needs are similar to the majority of those who participate in the project. Artistic activities have proven to be powerful antidotes to emotional distress, drug abuse, crime and violence. In fact, PSD has evolved into a model for treating a broad spectrum of teenage problems.

Substituting Art for Drugs

At PSD, you will find youth with varied backgrounds and behaviors. Betty Jo, a 15-year-old African American, describes her mother as "a bitch" and "evil," and Betty Jo has attempted suicide twice. Her art teacher says she is interacting nicely with other students and "demonstrates an orderly, precise and methodical way of working on projects."

Rosa, a 15-year-old Latina, has decided to never again "bang" with her sect of the gang Gangster Disciples. Five of her close friends have died or have been murdered during the past year. She is considered highly motivated by her music teacher.

The usual outcome for these kids is enormous frustration and definite failure. These teenagers have different types of mental disorders and behavioral problems and come from radically diverse backgrounds. In the United States 10% to 20% of the 30 million youths between ages 10 and 17 experience emotional and/or behavioral problems. Forty percent of their waking time is "discretionary." In fact, the majority of teenage crimes are committed between three in the afternoon and midnight. For these teenagers a form of positive self-expression is vital.

The inspiration for PSD came from viewing substance abuse as just one of many forms of dangerous pleasure-seeking behaviors. Any action that deposits dopamine [a chemical that induces feelings of pleasure] in the brain's reward center—be it alcohol, sex or cocaine—can trigger addiction. Yet rather than drugs, people can actually bring about self-induced changes in brain chemistry. The most important psychological challenge of our time is to bring about these changes through optimal living or natural highs.

Drugs and alcohol are really just "chemical prostitutes," counterfeit molecules that compromise the clockwork of nature's most complex and delicate entity—the human brain. According to the annual Monitoring the Future Survey, more than 40% of high-school 10th graders reported having "been drunk" sometime in the past year. About 35% of high school seniors engaged in binge drinking (having five or more drinks at a time), and approximately 20% of high school seniors smoked pot.

PSD was founded in September 1992 as the result of a national grant through the Center for Substance Abuse Prevention. The grant was awarded to Cleo Parker Robinson Dance, whose mission is to provide cross-cultural arts expression to audiences, artists and students. The project was designed to show that natural highs could serve as viable alternatives to drug abuse and associated high-risk lifestyles. Teenagers have been targeted because of their extreme vulnerability to substance abuse, crime and violence. The most common causes of death among young adults between ages 16 and 24 are homicide and suicide. Here, Juan talks about his brush with death:

> They came up the dirt hill. There were eight or nine of them and there was just six of us. My homeboy gave me a .25. It was already loaded, cocked and ready to bust some caps. So I went up to them and said, "I know you, the punk motherfucker who tagged up my locker. You disrespected my 'hood. Just kill me, motherfucker. Get it over with." So he pulls out this crowbar. And I pulled out the .25. I put it to his head and said, "What 'hood you from?" He said "CMG Blood." And I said "WHAT FUCKIN' 'HOOD YOU FROM?" And he said, "CMG Blood." Then he said, "Crip." I made that fool cry and shit. When you got a strap, you feel like you got the power to do anything in the world. You can make anybody scared of you with a strap.

While dance connects us to sensuality, music provides a safe vehicle for the expression of emotional unrest. Painting and drawing provide an opportunity to visualize topics initially too difficult for words. In Paula's script, it is evident that through writing and drama she is discovering important means to transcend the wounds of her childhood:

> He's my father. I don't even know what that means. I don't even know what a father is. I used to think he was someone who took me fishing, or maybe camping. Someone who I could talk to, who took care of me. But if you ask me, I'd say a father is someone who beats up his family. A father is someone who screams, yells and cusses out his family. A father is someone who breaks things, smashes things, ruins things. I HATE HIM. I HATE THIS HOUSE WHEN HE'S IN IT! It's like a war zone and he is the enemy. Every second, I'm looking over my shoulder to see if he's coming after me. He didn't tear up my drawings. He tore up my dreams. I HATE HIM! I hate it when he beats on my mom. I hate seeing my mother on the floor, I hate feeling like I have to protect her from the enemy and I HATE THAT THE ENEMY IS HIM. WHY AM I PROTECTING THE ENEMY? He's my father. I love him.

At-risk teens experience traditional talk therapies as invasive and persecutory. We have discovered that adventure-based counseling, hands-on games and physical challenges—like walking on stilts to "feel ten feet tall"—are far more engaging than standard lecture presentations. A kid who has a strong drive for thrill-seeking and novelty can avoid gang violence by satisfying his needs through the performance of poetry, hip-hop or rap. Almost magically, the conga, paintbrush or guitar can become formidable substitutes for pistols or joints.

It is no secret that people who are hopelessly dependent on drugs can still participate in the creative process. But the necessary complement to artistic development is learning to restructure habitual patterns of thought and feelings that trigger destructive actions. To this end all PSD youth participate in Pathways to Self Discovery, a 24-session life-skills curriculum. Teenagers discover improved means to cope with frustration, disappointment and anger.

David describes the course: "We gathered in a theater and talked about our past experiences with gangs, drugs and all the other things that teens face. We also talked about ways we could avoid these situations. I tried to be quiet, but my mouth would just shoot open. When it came to bad situations, I thought that I had a lot to offer the group."

David was making great progress. He had successfully embarked on the first stage of our three-tier program, each phase providing the foundation for the next level of growth and change. The three parts include the intervention program, the graduate program and the mentorship program. The last program allows graduate students, who have demonstrated leadership skills, to serve as facilitators and mentors to youth in the initial intervention program.

Another such course designed to transform is the Rites of Passage. In this adventure-based course, the kids are hooked up to a rope that's connected to a wire between two large poles. The object is to proceed from one end to the other. "The ropes course really scared me," says David. "I kept thinking, 'I am going to die.'"

When David hooked up his harness, though, everyone in the group started to cheer for him. "I got the strength to hurry through the course and when I got down, it felt as though a huge weight had been lifted off my shoulders."

Impressive Results

The results of PSD have been impressive. In the past nine years the project has received 1,255 referrals from Denver-area youth advocates. We have shown that artistic endeavor and adventure-based counseling are effective antidotes to drugs and other high-risk behaviors. Not only do participants show test scores reflecting improved mental health and family functioning, they also reveal decreased reliance on negative peer influences and decreased drug and alcohol use. These positive outcomes are sustained long after graduation.

As David puts it, because of PSD he has "become a better person." He has learned how to care for others and himself. "Without this experience, I would probably be living on the streets using drugs," he says. Today David shares a house with a friend, has a full-time job, and visits his mother once a week. He has also started boxing to relieve stress and lose weight. And for the last four years, he has been completely drug-free. He plans to go on to college and major in business and computer science. "PSD showed me that the world is full of possibilities. The program also showed me that when a door is closed a window is open. What does living mean to me now? Living is knowing that you are not alone."

PROVIDING TEENS WITH ALTERNATIVES TO GAMBLING

Jeffrey B. Zeiger and John J. Bullaro

As legalized casino gambling gains popularity throughout the United States, more and more teens are becoming compulsive gamblers. Jeffrey B. Zeiger and John J. Bullaro address this problem in the following selection, specifically concentrating on attempts by parks and recreation agencies to provide teens with alternatives to gambling. The authors find that gambling fulfills a variety of teens' social and personal needs, particularly their attraction to taking risks. By offering activities that appeal to thrill-seekers—such as rock climbing, ropes courses, or scuba diving—parks and recreation agencies can steer teens away from gambling, the authors maintain. Zeiger is the chair of the resource recreation and tourism program at the University of Northern British Columbia. Bullaro is a professor emeritus at the California State University at Northridge.

Legalized casino gambling has become one of America's favorite forms of recreation. According to a 1993 Yankelovich Partners study of 100,000 households, 27 percent had gambled at least once. Since 1992, 48 states have introduced legalized [casino] gambling (only Hawaii and Utah have not legalized gambling). Politicians from small, quiet towns across America dream of the surfeit of jobs, revenue, and new infrastructure in their communities—projects and employment that gaming operations might generate.

In June 1997, the Public Broadcasting Service's *Frontline* reported that Americans spend more money on gambling than on movies, theme parks, and live entertainment. In America, gaming revenue exceeds $500 billion a year. The number of casino-bound Americans doubled between 1994 and 1999. Las Vegas, America's fastest growing city, is the top destination resort in the country.

The nation's love affair with gambling is seducing a generation of teenagers, which is betting as much as $1 billion every year. Thanks to social support, gambling is rapidly becoming a bigger social problem than drugs for this age group. While teenage gambling is illegal in all states, studies reveal that adult behavior influences the choices young people make in their social responses to peer pressure.

Gambling's Impact on Youth

Henry Lesieur of Illinois State University estimates that in the United States 6 percent to 8 percent of teens between the ages of 13 and 17 are problem gamblers. These data, along with other statistics, suggest that recreation professionals face a critical new challenge: how to mitigate serious problems affecting teenage participation in an activity that is perfectly legal in the adult world. Lesieur's studies suggest that compulsive gambling among teens permeates our society. This position is echoed by Ken Winters, director of adolescent substance abuse at the University of Minnesota, who claims, "We're developing a generation of problem gamblers."

The tiny amount of information that is available on youth and gambling is not encouraging. In New Jersey, for example, problem-gambling hotline calls among youth jumped 200 percent between 1987 and 1993. A *USA Today* study published on April 5, 1995, reported that 90 percent of teenagers gambled before the age of 18, which suggests a surge in the future adult gambling population, a fact not overlooked by gaming-industry executives.

There are many challenges facing parks and recreation with respect to the problem of underage gambling. Gene Piscia, writing in *California Parks and Recreation* magazine in the summer of 1996, stated that the biggest challenge recreation agencies face is developing teen programs that work. This is a particularly poignant statement in light of the growth of gaming across the state. To address the issue of underage gambling, we must first understand its appeal to youth.

Armed with insight, it is possible to fashion program strategies for effective intervention. Studies suggest that when gambling is introduced into a community, illegal gambling among teens is certain to follow. Furthermore, these studies reveal that teens are twice as likely to be compulsive gamblers; 7 percent of teens under the age of 18 are deemed problem gamblers. A 1991 study by Lowell Caneday and Jeffrey B. Zeiger showed that residents' quality of life ultimately suffered when gambling and tourism came to town.

What Is Gambling's Appeal?

Gambling, in one form or another, is as American as apple pie. We use the office pool to gamble on sports. Churches have profitable bingo nights. Many states have legalized poker parlors. State lotteries stretch across the nation from coast to coast. So it appears our society agrees that under certain conditions, gambling is acceptable.

But why does gambling flourish? That gambling survives at all suggests that it meets social and personal needs of the gambler that are not being fulfilled otherwise. In an unpublished 1990 dissertation, researcher Edward C. Devereux of the University of Michigan concluded that gambling is successful because of the following characteristics:

1. Protest against budgetary constraints. The gambler, in a small way, can protest against the "tyranny of the budget" or lack of employment.
2. Protest against rationality. Too many of life's pleasures are controlled by rational thought. Gambling allows the gambler to strike a blow for personal freedom.
3. Protest against ethics. Not ethical in the gambler's mind, gambling provides a way of making a protest statement.
4. Thrill-seeking. Gambling helps to alleviate anxiety and boredom, which often accumulate as a result of ordinary activities.
5. Competitiveness and aggression. These emotions can be vented behind a "playful facade."
6. Problem-solving. Gambling, like crossword puzzles and chess (though with the additional contingency of the stake), provides artificial, short-term, miniature capsule problems—and their resolution—for those who cannot face or solve problems in real life.
7. Teleological motivation. Human search for meaning often takes place within the confines of the work (or school) environment. These environments do not put a premium on the "philosophical" or "intuitive" because these ideas are not supportive of goals of work or school. Gambling is the only popular arena in which notions of luck and superstition prevail.
8. Gambling is a social activity promoting access for anyone, including the shy youngster.

Teens Are Attracted to Risk

American popular culture has always courted and celebrated risk. America's young people, likewise, are attracted to risky pursuits: fast cars, drugs and alcohol, and contact sports. The Devereux study suggested that recreation intervention programs should be built upon the components of gaming's attraction. This notion holds promise for the development of positive diversionary recreation to replace gaming activity.

In the summer 1995 issue of *California Parks and Recreation,* Jay Beckwith suggested some excellent examples of risk recreation activities—rock climbing, ropes courses, BMX, and inline skating and hockey—which embody these components of gaming. Additional activities for diversionary programming might include climbing-wall competition, mountain-bike trips or races, cross-country endurance races, weightlifting contests, wilderness adventure trips, or scuba diving. Beckwith concludes his article by stressing that young people are attracted to activities with a high level of perceived risk.

As recreation professionals face shrinking budgets, losses in staff numbers, and growing responsibilities, the task of monitoring interest in gambling and the process of educating politicians and citizens about the benefits of recreation must find a place on crowded agendas. There are ways to deal with this challenge in the face of shrinking resources.

Community sharing of advisory-board influence and strategic planning can produce high-profile community activity, which could appeal to the media and politicians. No one agency should be expected to go it alone in the quest to gain funding for recreation and community service programs.

Volunteer community powerbrokers could be recruited to form an ad hoc committee to explore ways to influence the political process on behalf of recreation and other relevant community programs. Retired executives with years of organizational development experience can be recruited in most communities.

Properly recruited and motivated, a person with this background could assume a role of political action coordinator, relieving overworked and understaffed agencies of additional work. As gaming grows in popularity, this effort will become more and more crucial in the fight to meet parks and recreation's mission of service to youth.

PARENTS CAN PREVENT ADDICTION BY TALKING TO THEIR TEENS

Stacey Schultz

According to Stacey Schultz, many parents think they only need to tell their children not to use drugs one time for the message to get across. However, Schultz explains, once is not enough; teens need to hear the message repeatedly. Teens are more likely to place their confidence in their parents than in siblings, teachers, or friends, she notes, so parental advice about drugs can be highly effective. Parents need to educate themselves about drug use and the negative effects of substance abuse in order to communicate the anti-drug message effectively, the author writes. In addition, she stresses the need for parents to take effective action if they do discover that their teen is using drugs. Schultz is a staff writer for *U.S. News & World Report*, a weekly news magazine.

When Laura Langanki found extra towels in the laundry smelling lemony fresh, she never dreamed that meant her 13-year-old son was on drugs. "We were going through three to four bottles of air freshener a week," says the 42-year-old nurse from Plymouth, Minn. "Like a fool, I thought my kid was becoming more interested in personal hygiene." Instead, Jake was "huffing"—spraying the contents into towels and inhaling the fumes for a short-lived buzz. By the time she caught on two years later, he was smoking pot, using acid and crystal methamphetamine, drinking alcohol, and snorting cocaine.

Laura had warned Jake not to try illegal drugs when he was younger and felt sure he got the message. But according to a *U.S. News* poll, even parents who believe they talk often with their kids about drugs can be mistaken. Of 700 parents and 700 teens surveyed, 1 in 3 parents claimed to talk about drugs "a lot" with his or her teen, while only 14 percent of teenagers felt they had frequent conversations on the subject with Mom or Dad.

Parental Communication Is Key

That failure to communicate can have dire consequences. In a 1999 survey of nearly 10,000 parents and teens by the Partnership for a

Drug-Free America, teens who received antidrug messages at home were 42 percent less likely to use drugs. "This may sound like soft advice," says Steve Dnistrian, executive vice president of the group. "But hard numbers quantify that parental communication is the single most important thing we can do to prevent children from using drugs." Indeed, parents received the highest vote of confidence from 63 percent of the teens polled by *U.S. News*, outranking siblings, teachers, and friends.

Most teens act as if they would rather clean their room than talk to their parents about touchy subjects like drugs or sex. Don't be deterred, says Rhonda Sykes, associate clinical director for Hazelden Chicago, a drug treatment center for adolescents. "Teens don't say, 'Thanks for the great advice.' But they do hear what their parents are saying."

Brandi Domiano, a 16-year-old from Old Forge, Pa., who has never tried cigarettes or alcohol, credits her mother for the choices she makes now. "When I was in sixth grade, my mother would talk to me about how bad drinking and smoking are for you," Domiano says. Her mother also gave her books to read about the harmful effects of drugs.

Talking to Kids About Drugs

Experts agree conversations about drugs should begin early and continue throughout adolescence. "Start talking about it when the child is around age 8," says Richard Gallagher, director of the Parenting Institute at New York University Child Study Center. Explain the difference between legal drugs prescribed by doctors and illegal drugs used for fun. Let your children know that other kids may offer these substances to them and that you want them to stay away from drugs because of the harmful effects on health and well-being, Gallagher says.

Many parents will have to do homework on the dangers of drugs. "The only thing worse than no information is bad information," says Paul Ciborowski, professor of counseling at Long Island University's C.W. Post campus. Ask youth counselors and teachers which drugs are common at your child's school so you can emphasize the right ones. The Internet can provide research on the ill effects of certain drugs.

Resist the temptation to lecture. Ask lots of questions, and listen to your child's opinions and feelings. And make sure your kids get the message that you're talking about the topic because you're concerned and you want them to be safe.

Kids may fire back with the dreaded question: "Did you do drugs when you were young?" "No need to let it all hang out," Ciborowski says. Be honest, but don't spell out everything. Stress lessons you learned, and talk about people you knew who had a hard time because they used drugs. "Real stories of people who were separated from their families or had to do jail time are what keep me off drugs," says Thomas Brennan, 16, of New York City.

If there is alcoholism in the family, you need to explain to your children that they are at higher risk, says Sandra Bernabei, a substance abuse specialist at Barnard College. That's what Alex Benson's parents did. "I definitely think about it and it scares me," says the 15-year-old from Springfield, Vt. "My uncle is an alcoholic and I know that one day it could be me."

Assumptions and Consequences

Bernabei also warns parents not to assume that all kids use drugs. According to findings from the University of Michigan Institute for Social Research, 55 percent of high school seniors say they have tried illicit drugs. In the past year, close to 40 percent smoked marijuana, almost 6 percent used inhalants, 8 percent took LSD, 6 percent used cocaine, 1 percent took heroin, and close to 6 percent say they used MDMA, also known as Ecstasy. "The truth is, a minority of kids use drugs or binge drink regularly," Bernabei says. Conveying the idea that all kids use drugs may make your child feel pressure to join in. And parents aren't the only ones guilty of exaggerating; 25 percent of the teenagers in our poll said most teens use drugs on a regular basis. But only 8 percent said close friends are frequent users.

At the same time, don't assume that your child is not being exposed. According to a study from researchers at Columbia University, teens in small towns and rural areas are far more likely to use drugs than urban kids. "It's not about boredom, it's about monitoring," says NYU's Gallagher, who explains that rural and small-town kids can find lots of secluded hangouts.

It's also about consequences. When kids say, "My parents will kill me if I use drugs," they really don't know what will happen. Experts advise parents to make it clear that even one infraction will bring a punishment—something with teeth, but still reasonable, like a temporary grounding. If parents learn that a child is using drugs habitually, they need to seek treatment.

Ultimately, your child will decide whether to try drugs, and even the best parents cannot always prevent it. But don't give up. Once Laura Langanki became aware of Jake's drug use she battled back, spending her savings to get him into a residential rehabilitation program. At 18, he just celebrated his 18th month of sobriety. When asked to complete an essay assignment on a significant person in his life, he chose to write about his mom.

CHAPTER 4

TEENS' PERSONAL STORIES OF ADDICTION AND RECOVERY

Contemporary Issues
Companion

THE TALE OF A SEVENTEEN-YEAR-OLD SMOKER

Edwin Mercado

Edwin Mercado was seventeen years old when he wrote this personal narrative of his path to cigarette addiction. He explains that he hated smoking at first, but he soon began to crave the addictive rush brought on by nicotine. When Mercado's mother first discovered that he smoked, her anger and disappointment prompted him to try to stop for a while. But even the punishment and lectures he faced could not break him of his habit, he relates. Mercado admits that he is addicted to tobacco and needs to quit because his habit is already adversely affecting his health. He says that he will do whatever it takes to overcome his addiction to cigarettes, but he realizes that it will be a difficult task.

I smoked my first cigarette when I was 12. My father, who smokes, was cleaning up the day after a party. He lit a cigarette, took two drags and just left it in the ashtray.

When he left the room to go to sleep, I saw my opportunity. It was a spur of the moment thought. "Edwin, take a drag," I said to myself.

I guess I wanted to try it because just about everyone in my family smokes or used to smoke: my father, mother, grandfather, aunts, uncles and my older sister. Then I thought, "But what if you get caught?" I was going crazy wondering whether I should take a drag.

I Hated It at First

I finally decided to go for it, so I took about five drags of the cigarette.

My first impression of smoking was terrible. The taste was nasty and I felt like throwing up.

But there was something about it I liked. Smoking made me get a lightheaded rush and that felt kind of good. I wanted to feel that same rush again.

So I started stealing cigarettes from my father and smoking them in my room or the bathroom.

I was soon smoking about four cigarettes a day, but it wasn't until I turned 14 that I started buying cigarettes. Since I started getting a whole bunch of facial hair, I looked old enough to buy them.

I didn't have much money, so I had to buy loosies, which until 1999 cost 25 cents for one cigarette. It became a habit, buying about three cigarettes in the morning and three after school. Since I was 14—I'm 17 now—I've hardly gone a day without smoking a cigarette, except when I'm sick. I'm addicted.

Getting Caught by Mom

It's been hard to hide my smoking from my parents, because I want to smoke when I'm home.

The first time I got caught, it was because I had left cigarettes in my pocket. I had bought one and taken one each from my mother and grandfather.

My mom had come into my room one morning to wake me up for school. She saw my jeans. "You want me to wash these?" she asked. Without thinking, I said yes, so she emptied out my pockets and that's when she found the cigarettes.

I was brushing my teeth when she barged into the bathroom and said in a loud, scary mother voice, "What the f-ck is this?"

I dropped the tooth brush. "Ahh, sh-t," I said. "They're not mine, I found them."

"Yeah, right," she said and smacked me hard upside my head.

When my mother gets angry, it's not a pretty sight. Her face gets red and her lips turn smaller and it scares the hell out of me.

That whole day I was in shock because she caught me and I didn't know what to do.

It was the worst feeling in the world when my mother found out I was smoking. I felt like the world was going to end.

When I got caught, I thought about stopping. I did stop for about a week, because all I could think about was getting caught again. But I got a little less worried, and I started up again.

I wish I had my Mom's willpower. When my mother used to smoke, she smoked about four cigarettes a day. She didn't really like it, but it became a habit. One day she said, "That's it for me; I'm going to stop smoking."

And she did. Within a week she had stopped totally. My father, though, has been smoking for over 20 years. He always says he's going to stop, but he doesn't.

My parents have caught me about five times with a cigarette in my mouth and about 30 times by finding cigarette butts in my room or in the laundry room. I get screamed at and punished.

As punishment for smoking, my parents don't give me money for a while. Plus, I've gotten about 100 lectures, where they ask "Where do you get your cigarettes from?" or say "I'm going to kick your ass if you keep on smoking."

I've heard it all, so now I lie to save myself the lectures. When I

leave butts around or have a cigarette smell when I come out of the
bathroom, I just deny it.

I've tried to smoke outside my house but when I come back, my
parents ask me, "Where were you?" I say, "I needed some fresh air."
They know I'm lying. I can see it in their eyes; they look at me as if
I'm stupid.

I feel real bad when I have a hard time with my parents, and I tell
myself I'm not going to smoke anymore, but I still do.

Smoking Makes Me Sick

I think my parents don't want me to smoke because they know how
hard it can be to stop. And they don't want me to try smoking other
things like weed.

I know smoking is bad for me because I'm only 17 and I can't even
play three games of basketball. I usually have to stop because I can't
breathe. I don't want to be in the hospital in 10 years, coughing up
phlegm because I'm a smoker.

Smoking already makes me sick. From time to time, I get a sore
throat that feels like I swallowed glass.

When I get this sore throat, I tell myself I'm going to stop smoking
but all I do is cut down. And when my sore throat is gone, I start
smoking as much as before. As I write this, I'm getting a sore throat. It
makes me want to stop, but I keep smoking anyway.

Smoking is also bad for my wallet. The first day I found out that
they raised the prices for cigarettes, I felt like crying since I now go
through a pack in about two days, three at the most.

Packs of cigarettes used to cost $3.25 or $3.50, and now they cost
$4.25 or $4.50. Some places in Manhattan charge $5.25. (I also buy
three packs of Doublemint every day so my breath won't stink.)

I know I'm wasting my money on something like that, because I
know smoking isn't good for me, but I can't stop. I don't think I could
go a day without having a cigarette. What I like about smoking is that
it calms me down. If I'm pissed off about something, I just smoke a
cigarette and I'm not so mad.

When I don't have a cigarette, I get very cranky. And I don't know
why, but my stomach starts to crave food. I could have just finished
eating, but I get hungry. It's not a good feeling.

Planning to Quit

A few of my friends smoke, but they're not addicted like me. They
only smoke sometimes. They tell me "Yo Ed, you need to stop smoking. You gonna just die one of these days." I tell them, "Yeah, I need
to stop, but I can't."

I know there are patches and gum that supposedly help you stop
smoking.

I haven't tried those patches or gum myself, but I know people who say it's a waste of time and money. I think if you really want to stop smoking, you have to do it on your own.

I plan to stop smoking soon, maybe by January; I'll make that my New Year's resolution.

I plan to stop little by little, maybe cutting down at first to about three cigarettes a day. But if that doesn't work, I'll go cold turkey. I know if I go cold turkey I'm going to go through some hard times, because I'm going to have the urge to smoke, but I'm going to do whatever it takes to stop.

CHEWING TOBACCO: A YOUNG ATHLETE'S DANGEROUS ADDICTION

Claire Martin

In the following selection, Denver Post *staff reporter Claire Martin relates the experience of Mike Watson, a high school baseball player struggling to overcome his addiction to chewing tobacco. Mike believed that since famous athletes use chewing tobacco, it must not be dangerous, Martin explains. But after only three years of using, he was diagnosed with precancerous lesions in his mouth. Mike acknowledges that he is addicted and scared, but even the threat of cancer has not been enough to enable him to quit. Martin writes that Mike is currently trying to break his addiction with the help of a program designed by a tobacco cessation expert; however, she cautions that tobacco chewing is one of the most difficult addictions to overcome.*

Leukoplakia. Pre-cancerous lesions, announced Mike Watson's orthodontist after inspecting the 17-year-old boy's mouth.

Watson clings to those three letters—pre—like a mantra.

"Pre-cancerous," he will say, carefully emphasizing the prefix.

He is tall, athletic, and good-looking, with broad shoulders already filling out his letterman's jacket.

He looks at himself in the mirror and finds it hard to imagine that someday the cancer will eat away that prefix, along with his jaw, his tongue and, if he won't quit, his life.

"I've always been good," he will say, meaning that he doesn't drink, do drugs or smoke cigarettes. And meaning, how could someone so healthy and young be threatened by a disease that belongs to old people?

Watson is still a kid, impulsive enough to bleach his dark hair just because the rest of the guys decided that everyone on the ball team should have bleached hair.

"I had worries," he will say, "that it might be somewhat dangerous. But . . . "

But big-league baseball players use chewing tobacco. Watson started dipping, at age 13, because he wanted to look like his favorite ball player, former Rockies first baseman Andres Galarraga. Galarraga chewed.

Watson knew other kids who surreptitiously dipped. (Of the 12 million Americans who use chewing tobacco, one-third are under age 21, according to *The Tobacco Almanac,* and nearly 16 percent of the boys in grades nine through 12 use chewing tobacco.)

And it's called "smokeless" tobacco. He figured, how bad could it be? Certainly not as bad as cigarettes, right?

Chewing Tobacco Is Dangerous

"I think the word 'smokeless,' the guy who came up with that, he deserves a bonus; in one word, he makes it sound harmless," said Joe Garagiola, the broadcaster and former St. Louis Cardinals catcher who has made a personal cause of campaigning against what he calls "spit tobacco."

"'Smokeless,' Garagiola added, "does not mean 'harmless.'"

Watson first learned that in 1997. When he was a freshman on the Thunder Ridge High School baseball team in Denver, Colorado, chest pains sent him into convulsions. The school nurse called Donald Watson, and he took his son to the hospital.

"Mike spent five days there while they tested him for everything in the world," his father said.

The diagnosis: An ulcerated esophagus.

"You chew tobacco?" the doctor asked. It wasn't really a question.

Mike Watson paused. He knew it was illegal for a minor to dip.

"A little," he said at last. "Once in a while."

The doctor gave him a long look. Better quit, he said.

On the way home, Donald Watson was frustrated. Knock that crap off, he told his son. Mike Watson promised he would.

"I thought about quitting then," he said later, "but as soon as I got out of the hospital, it was too hard. I couldn't do it. It is sad to say that a 16-year-old could be addicted to spit tobacco," Watson says, "but . . ."

But he went through a half-can of Copenhagen a day. Still does.

Chewing Tobacco Is Easy to Get

It is much easier, he has learned, for a teenager to buy tobacco for four years than it is to quit using it. He knows to the penny what convenience stores charge for a can of Copenhagen.

"Three-ninety-seven," Watson says, without checking the can.

He also knows that most clerks don't bother to read the identification cards they ask to see. Before he got his driver's license, Watson used his Thunder Ridge High School student card as an ID when he bought Skoal. Almost as soon as he got his driver's license, he used it, unaltered, to buy a new can of tobacco.

It is ridiculously easy, he says, to circumvent the Colorado law that makes it illegal to sell tobacco, in any form, to a minor.

It was almost as easy to hide his habit from his parents, his teachers and his coaches. He was careful to hide his can in his sock, where it didn't show. He stashed the empties in an old headphones box he kept in his closet. Not even his dentist suspected Mike dipped.

One time, his dad found a can of tobacco in Mike's truck. Donald Watson confronted his son. Mike claimed it belonged to his friends. He promised that it would never happen again.

In March 1999, in his son's bedroom, Donald Watson found an empty Skoal can full of tobacco juice. He lectured Mike again. Two days later, he opened his sock drawer and found a folded piece of notebook paper labeled "DAD."

"Please don't hate me," Mike wrote, "I understand if you want to take the truck away." He wrote that he didn't want to hide the fact that he was chewing tobacco, that he felt guilty using his parents' money to finance his habit—and that he didn't think he'd be quitting soon.

"That evening, Mike said to me, 'It's not like smoking, Dad; you don't get lung cancer from this,'" Donald Watson said.

"That was the thought in his mind—it wasn't all that bad. I started talking about Clark Gable and Curt Schilling, and other people who chew who had cancer. I couldn't understand why someone who enjoyed sports would jeopardize his body like that."

It didn't really sink in until the following Monday, when the dentist found the lesion in Mike Watson's mouth.

"When he said, 'It's pre-cancerous tissue,' my heart started pumping a little quicker," Mike Watson said.

Trying to Quit

The Watsons met with Thunder Ridge baseball coaches Dave Mumpher and Joe White, who had no idea that Mike chewed.

They showed him *The Bob Leslie Story*, a video about a baseball coach who, like Mike, began chewing when he was 13. Leslie was diagnosed with oral cancer before he was 28 and lost most of his lower lip and jaw. He died in the summer of 1998. He was 31.

They gave him a copy of *What's Really in Spit Tobacco*, a brochure shaped like a tobacco can. It includes a picture of Sean Marsee, who started using chew when he was 12. Marsee died of oral cancer at age 19.

They suspended him for two games, as a penalty for chewing.

Mike still couldn't quit.

"I've gone, like, five or six hours without a chew, but I can't go longer than that," he said.

"I've tried stopping, but it is just not happening."

Exasperated, his mother, Cheryl, called the number on one of the brochures that the coaches gave Mike and talked to Dave Avrin, the local publicist for the National Spit Tobacco Education Program (NSTEP).

Avrin was sympathetic. He offered an idea: If Mike Watson speaks out against chewing tobacco, Avrin said, we'll put you in touch with the best cessation experts in the country.

A week later, Mike Watson and his parents were standing next to Joe Garagiola at an NSTEP press conference at Dodger Stadium in Los Angeles. Mike made a speech about his addiction. He announced that his goal was to quit by Sept. 10, 1999, his 18th birthday.

"It took a lot of guts to do that," Garagiola said.

"He said something like, 'I started when I was 13 and I was real cool, the cool kid on the block, and here I am, four years later, and there's nothing cool about it. I'm addicted.' That takes a lot of guts, man."

A week after the press conference, Mike threw his can of Copenhagen out the window. He went all weekend without a chew. On Monday, he was dipping again.

"Guys tell me that quitting spit tobacco is the toughest thing they've ever done," said Garagiola.

"And one had experience with cocaine. Some guys get off it, then get back on it. It is addictive."

In May 1999, Mike and his parents had a teleconference with Herb Severson, a leading cessation expert and author. Severson set up a program designed to wean Mike from chewing tobacco by May 26.

"It will be a lot of work," Cheryl Watson said.

"The nicotine will be out of his body in a week, but withdrawal takes two weeks. Psychologically, it lasts longer: Your body is programmed physiologically to put that chew in. And Mike is at the high end of the addiction scale, according to Dr. Severson."

In early May, he began the withdrawal program, starting by shifting from Copenhagen (79 percent nicotine) to Skoal (28 percent nicotine). Just before he quits on May 26, he'll be down to Hawken (7 to 10 percent nicotine).

"It's definitely different: You don't get the same effect," Mike Watson said. He compared it to the difference between regular soda and diet soda.

"I feel more tired and stuff. But I'm quitting on May 26. I knew I was pretty addicted, but I didn't know I was at the higher end of it. I've learned a lot of stuff in the past couple weeks. My goal is to play college baseball, and if that's my dream, then I've got to do what's right and not chew."

Two Teens Speak Out on Their Struggles with Alcohol

Kerri Dowd

In the following selection, Kerri Dowd interviews two teenage girls who became hooked on alcohol at a young age. Angela Mendell came from a family of alcoholics and drug users, but she started drinking primarily because of curiosity and peer influence. Desiree Suarez, on the other hand, began drinking in search of emotional solace from problems in her family. However, both girls agree that alcohol soon took over their lives. In Angela's case, Dowd writes, a series of personal tragedies related to alcohol and substance abuse were the catalyst she needed to stop drinking. For Desiree, it was the support offered from friends at church that finally helped her to quit. Dowd is a victim advocate and newsletter editor for the King County, Washington, chapter of Mothers Against Drunk Driving.

Angela and Desiree saw drinking as a ticket to popularity and a way to deal with their problems. Sure, they'd heard the facts from counselors, classes, and awareness programs, but they didn't believe or care. Now, after years of alcohol abuse, they talk about what got them started, what helped them stop, and what you can do to help a friend with a drinking problem.

Angela's Battle with Alcohol

Angela Mendell is 19 now, but she took her first drink when she was 13. From then until she was 17 she drank heavily, especially on weekends.

Although her mother and stepfather were drug users and her stepfather was an alcoholic, Angela didn't see them as a major influence in her drinking.

Angela doesn't feel it was peer pressure that got her started either. She says, "It was more peer influence. It wasn't like anyone was saying, 'Here, try this.' I asked. I was curious, and my friends happened to have it."

Angela says her drinking had more effect on her emotions than it did on her outward life. Shuffled from relative to relative, she was

Reprinted from "When the Party's Over," by Kerri Dowd, *Listen*, February 1999, by permission of the author.

usually able to cover her activities, which eventually included smoking cigarettes and marijuana and experimenting with other drugs. The family members who found out pretty much left her to work through the issue on her own. She was keeping up with her grades, and her teachers liked her. No one knew she was a party girl. "I was living two separate lives. My reputation at school was pretty good. In the community I played the role of being little Goody Twoshoes."

By the time she was a junior, though, Angela was having trouble at school, but she kept insisting it wasn't the alcohol. It was everything else in her life that was falling apart. She was seriously behind in the number of credits she needed and had to go to an alternative school to catch up. School hours there were from 7:00 A.M. to 6:00 P.M., and Angela made up 16 credits in one year.

Getting a Wake-Up Call

She never went through a formal recovery program to get help with her drinking problem. Instead, three key events helped her wake up to what she was doing to herself. The first was when she was 16. "One of my best friends was killed," she remembers. "I guess he was going to get ice cream, and two guys shot him for his clothes. The thing that really made me straighten up was that I knew the two guys who killed him. I had partied with them."

Angela's second wake-up call was the drug-related murder of her stepfather just before her senior year.

The third event—maybe the clincher—was simply her best friend's disappointment in her. "We'd been best friends since I was 6. I knew how she felt about what I was doing without her having to tell me. But because she didn't tell me, I ignored how I knew she felt. When she finally did tell me how disappointed she was, it almost killed me because she's the person I cherish most in life.

"She just told me that she knows I'm smarter than that and that I could have a lot going on for me. She said that she cares about me and that I had better potential."

Angela says the combination of everything—needing to get focused, her friend getting killed, and her dad dying—made her realize she didn't need to be doing this stuff. She quit drinking, getting high, and smoking all at once.

Part of Angela's self-styled recovery is her involvement in a group called SWAY (Southwest Alliance for Youth), a Seattle, Washington, youth council that brings kids together from all walks of life to help other youths and to help the community. Angela and the others have worked on gathering clothes for homeless people, cooking meals at a homeless shelter, putting on drug- and alcohol-free entertainment, and painting a mural for a bus shelter.

Maybe as a natural consequence, Angela rediscovered a value system. "I still went to church when I was drinking," Angela says. "I was just kind of lost at the time. My faith wasn't so much an issue in getting me straightened up, but as I got straightened up, I became a stronger Christian."

Angela graduated from high school and is engaged to be married. She says, "Drinking and using drugs is fun and games for a while, but you have to realize that you have to grow up sometime. Even if you may not personally get hurt, it hurts the people around you."

Desiree's Story

Desiree Suarez is 18. She recently celebrated one year of sobriety. She started drinking the summer before her freshman year of high school. And later she started taking drugs.

Her parents were going through a divorce. "I couldn't find security in my family," she says. "Just hearing them yelling and hearing the problems they were going through . . . you just don't want to deal with it. When you're having problems, you just want to go do something. I figured the drinking would be a little baby step. I thought it would take care of my problems. That's the reason most teens want to go and smoke and drink. It takes you out of your own world for a few hours."

Desiree says another reason she drank was to be popular. "Being an incoming freshman, you just want to be down with a clique, down with their friends. That's where the hip hop is, and that's what really drags you in."

For three years Desiree was heavily into that scene—drinking, smoking, and doing drugs. She lived with her father, who didn't know what was happening at first. "It's so easy to do this without letting your parents know, because I guess you could say that we kids have connections—adults who are willing to buy the alcohol, friends who have it, mini-markets that sell it. Neither of my parents knew until I got caught at school."

Alcohol Messes Up People's Lives

While talking about what her drinking did to her life, Desiree's tone changes. She wants to nail the point. "Oh, man," she says. "If I could go back. . . . It totally messed up my life." She says the alcohol and marijuana made her react slowly. "You don't even care what's happening anymore. It made me not go to school anymore. It's not really you. The alcohol starts controlling you."

She says she doesn't remember much about high school. "All I know is I'm going to graduate and get my diploma." She regrets missing out on the learning. Her grades were affected, and she lost a lot of credits. "It made my transcript look really, really bad. I'm trying to make a life right now, but it will follow me everywhere I go."

It's hard now for Desiree to study, and she has trouble focusing. "I've been clean for a long time, but it's like I read a page and I totally forget what I just read." When people explain how to do something, such as use a machine, Desiree needs to actually go through the motions. Verbal instructions are not enough.

Deep into her addiction her father told her to stop. Some of her friends nagged. The drug and alcohol counselor at her school sent her to a drug-awareness program and set her up with a counselor, who checked up on her once or twice a week.

Desiree doesn't credit any of these efforts with setting her straight. She says what made the difference was some people at her church stepping up and saying, "We care about you, and so does God."

Her advice for dealing with a friend who has a problem: "Don't always nag about it. Always remember that actions are more powerful than words. Having a friend who would say 'Hey, let's go to a movie' or 'Let's go talk to someone about it' really helps." The key, she says, is not just to say you care, but to back that up by being willing to spend time with the person, being loving, and by showing that you're there for them.

That's what Desiree's church friends did. They told her they wanted to hang with her, and they really took time out to be with her. Even now when she sees kids at school whom she knows are using, she will pull them aside and talk to them one by one. But she has bigger plans. "After college I'm going to try to work at community centers. I've been there, done that, and I can make a difference."

THE HIGHEST OF HIGHS: MY ADDICTION TO HEROIN

Caroline, as told to Gary L. Somdahl

A young woman named Caroline discusses her addiction to heroin and her journey toward recovery in the following selection. Caroline explains that she never took drugs until she was sixteen, when her parents announced their separation. She was so emotionally devastated by the end of her parents' marriage that she started using drugs to numb her pain. After working her way through several drugs, Caroline relates, she became addicted to heroin at seventeen. Her school principal eventually recognized that Caroline had a drug problem and told her parents. With the help of drug rehabilitation and therapy, Caroline freed herself from addiction. Gary L. Somdahl is a licensed youth chemical dependency counselor and the author of *Listen* magazine's "Ask Gary" column.

At 16 I was a lot like most kids my age. I had the usual problems with boys, school, zits, parents, and almost everything that drives us all nuts. You could say I was a typical teen with the typical dream to be somebody someday. That was before I became attracted to drugs. That was before I became hooked on heroin.

Like you, I'm sure, I had always been taught the boring reasons nobody should ever consider getting stoned. It doesn't take a rocket scientist to figure out that drugs can screw up a life and, even worse, kill. And at first I heeded the warnings. I kept as far away from them as I could. That is, until something crazy happened in my life a few months before my seventeenth birthday.

A Family Crisis

It happened one evening while I was watching one of those tearjerker romance movies at home with my parents. With no warning they nonchalantly brought up the fact that they'd decided to go their separate ways for a while. Instead of trying to work things out, they figured that time apart was going to make things better. To say I was surprised would be the understatement of the year. I was in shock and

Reprinted from "Seventeen and Hooked," by Gary L. Somdahl, *Listen*, December 1999, by permission of the author.

scared half out of my wits. I remember going over the top end on the anger scale and raising my voice.

"How could you both do this to me? What about our family? What about me?" That's when I grabbed my coat and stormed out the door. I must have walked in circles for hours. It felt as if my entire life was being sucked down the toilet. I kept thinking, Who will I live with? What should I do? Where will I go?

Lonely, hungry, and shivering from the cold, I plowed through the snow to my friend Heather's house. My parents had forbidden me to see her since they discovered she was sort of a troublemaker and mostly preoccupied with getting high. Rumor around school was that she was a pipeline for anyone wishing to buy dope. I didn't care. At that moment I would have leaned on the shoulder of a mass murderer if one had been near.

You can probably guess what happened next. She turned me on to pot. Of course I felt some shame and guilt after the first hit. But it went up in smoke with each puff I took. The buzz was nothing like when I'd sneaked a couple sips from my dad's beer when I was 7. It didn't take too long before I was as relaxed as a rag doll, seemingly without a worry in the world.

The next month my folks split, and I stayed with my mom. I saw my dad every weekend until he moved out of town. That was when I began getting zoned out of my skull nearly every day. Booze, pot, pills—it was all the same! It didn't matter what it was, as long as it helped me escape into my own private world: the place I felt the safest. I figured I could always quit when things got better. Though something told me they never would.

Searching for a More Powerful High

My tolerance increased with every drug I tried, and the results were never as satisfactory as before. It left me searching for something different, something new, something more powerful. I began chasing after the highest of the highs. Heroin filled this need.

Who ever would have thought that someone so afraid of needles would end up slamming one of the most dangerous and deadly drugs into their veins? It was a friend of a friend of a friend who introduced me. By that time I was hanging with a crowd of rebels I would have avoided like the plague before.

His name was Gerry, and he was 25. Since most of my trusted friends had parted ways, he was someone who understood and listened. He also supplied the tools to get high—but for a price. I went against my better judgment and allowed him to take advantage of me any way he saw fit. When you're under the thumb of stuff that changes your mood and your mind, logic and reasoning take a hike. Besides, trading my body was no big deal. I would have sold my soul if I could.

Initially shooting up was nerve-racking, disgusting, and horrid. The only way I got through it was to close my eyes and pretend I was dreaming as the warm brown liquid plunged into my arm. The effects were like nothing I had ever felt before. The hair bristled on the back of my neck. My body and mind went totally numb. From that instant on, I set a new goal. As sick as it sounds, it was to stay loaded for the rest of my life. For quite a time afterward I chased the "dragon," as it's called. Obviously I was hooked; but an addict is always the last one to know. The high school principal was the first.

"Caroline," he told me, "I've been in this business enough years to recognize a drug problem blindfolded." I tried to choke back the tears and appear as though nothing was wrong. It was no use. The drug had taken its toll. It had become the master and had made me its slave. Sick and tired of always being sick and tired, I broke down and bawled.

Getting Help

My mother didn't believe it at first. They say an addict is pretty skilled at keeping those closest to them from ever finding out. I had to show her practically every abscessed area where the needle made its mark. I remember her throwing up after seeing the red festering wounds on my arms. She called my father, and he drove in the next day.

After an appointment with the family doctor, it was agreed I'd enter a drug rehab program near Seattle. It was scary at first. Not so much the part about learning to lead a clean and sober life, but the loss of a friend. Heroin had become my best pal. There are times I still grieve for it and probably will for quite a while yet.

Twenty-eight days later, after hours of group therapy, education, assignments, videos, lectures, and having to share my most intimate secrets, I walked out those doors a changed person. I realize now how close I came to losing my life, and how easy it could be to go back to the old ways. But I don't intend to. I never want to live that way again.

It's too bad that all other teens can't understand the wicked way of drugs. I wish they could comprehend that no one is immune from becoming hooked. Even after just one try. It's the old "It won't happen to me" syndrome. I thought the same. And I'll admit I was wrong.

An important lesson I've learned is to accept life on life's terms. Nothing is ever as bad as it seems. And it certainly can never be as bad as the results from falling headfirst into the web of drugs. I know, because I was there.

Today I still live with my mother and have a great relationship with my father. I've come to the conclusion that some things are out of my control and impossible to change. What I can change is my attitude and the way I view life.

I'm grateful to be back to my typical self and facing the same problems as most teens my age. There is nothing so bad that a drug won't make it worse. There is nothing so bad as addiction.

LOSING EVERYTHING TO COMPULSIVE GAMBLING

Bob Hugel

In the following selection, Bob Hugel relates the story of Lisa Hoffman, who began gambling when she turned eighteen—the legal age for gambling in her home state of Idaho. As Hugel recounts, Lisa's gambling activity soon turned into a full-blown addiction, one that she was willing to lie and steal to maintain. Even when Lisa realized she had a problem, the author writes, she could not stop herself from going to the casino and gambling away the money she had stolen from her father and her job. When Lisa was fired from her job for stealing, her parents finally realized the extent of her problem. With their help and treatment from Gamblers Anonymous, Lisa overcame her addiction and is working to rebuild her life. Hugel writes for *Scholastic Choices* magazine.

Lisa Hoffman of Moscow, Idaho, had long looked forward to turning 18. In her eyes and the world's, she was now an adult. Better still, she had finally reached the legal gambling age in her state.

Lisa's mom gambled and so did her grandparents. Her grandfather had once declared bankruptcy, in part because of his gambling debts, Lisa says. Still, in her family, gambling was considered an exciting and potentially profitable activity. "Growing up, I'd hear that I'd get to go to casinos or play bingo for money when I turned 18," Lisa recalls.

So, on the night of her 18th birthday, Lisa, full of anticipation, drove to the Nez Percé Indian reservation 30 miles from home. With her boyfriend, Rob, she strolled through the door of the Clearwater River Casino, into a plain room filled with video-game slot machines. Lights and colored displays flashed invitingly. Bells and buzzers sounded, and Lisa felt like a winner.

A Destructive Urge

When she left the casino that night, Lisa was short a mere $5. But she brought home an urge to gamble that grew into a destructive addiction. Within a year, she had gambled away several thousand dollars and lost the trust of her family. "Gambling," Lisa admits, "took over my life."

Lisa isn't alone. Today, nearly two out of three teenagers gamble, according to the National Council on Problem Gambling, a nonprofit group based in Columbia, Maryland. That's a 17 percent increase from the early 1980s, estimates the council, when about 50 percent of teens gambled. Most teen gamblers play cards occasionally with their friends, buy lottery tickets, or participate in Super Bowl pools. But about 1.1 million U.S. teenagers gamble compulsively, according to research by the National Academy of Sciences.

Compulsive gamblers are those who feel they can't stop themselves from betting. To feed their habit, they may lie, cheat, steal, or neglect their responsibilities. "It's vital that the public, especially teenagers, be made more aware that gambling can be harmful," says Dr. Durand F. Jacobs, clinical psychiatrist and spokesperson for the National Council on Problem Gambling.

At first, Lisa's gambling paid off. "Frequently, I'd go to the casino with $20 and walk out with $300 or $400," she says. "I didn't have a lot of money, and so it was a big thrill."

Lisa was experiencing the early stage of a gambling problem. Compulsive gambling often begins with "a big win or wins," explains Laura Letson, executive director of the New York Council on Problem Gambling, a nonprofit group. "It feels so good, they keep gambling."

Mounting Losses

Lisa's winning stage lasted about four months. By then, however, she had started spending all of her free time at the casino. She'd go there alone, spend a few hours, return home, pick up her mom or a friend, and return to the casino, pretending she hadn't been there already. She had entered what experts call the losing stage, and her losses were mounting. "I'd win a jackpot every now and then," Lisa says. "But every bit of money I won went back into the slot machines." That included $600 she had received as a high school graduation gift.

Although Lisa earned some money from a part-time job at a deli, it wasn't enough to pay for her gambling habit. As she reached the desperation stage—the final step to becoming a compulsive gambler—she began cashing bad checks.

Lisa also stole from her father, a farmer who sometimes had a great deal of cash on hand. "I took hundreds of dollars at a time from his wallet, without him noticing," she says. "I'd rationalize that if I won money gambling, I'd pay the people I owed. But the money I won, I gambled away. Afterward, I'd sit in my car, cry, and beat my head against the steering wheel. I couldn't believe I had done it again. But by the next day, I'd tell myself it was my turn to win."

The bank sent letters home, and Lisa's father discovered her thefts. Confrontations became weekly events. Lisa would cry, apologize, and promise to stop gambling. She couldn't. Her father hid his wallet, and he and Lisa's mom tried hiding and, eventually, burning Lisa's checkbook, but not until after she racked up $1,400 in debts from fraudulent checks. "My parents' friends told them that they should let me go to jail," Lisa says. "But they couldn't let me fall that far. They were hoping that I'd wake up, realize what I was doing, and get help."

Not About Winning

Lisa's obsession translated into physical symptoms—also typical of compulsive gamblers. "Gambling made me sick," she says. "I started getting migraine headaches." In addition, Lisa says, several times she arrived at the casino without clearly knowing how she had gotten there. She stopped caring how she looked and dressed.

"After a while, I didn't even care if I won or lost," she says, echoing a common attitude among compulsive gamblers. As Letson confirms, "At some point, it's not about winning anymore. It's about getting a fix from making a bet."

But even the act of betting was wearing thin. "I hated to be there, but I could not stop going to the casino," Lisa says. "It was the worst feeling. I felt so helpless."

In November 1997, a year after she fed her first dollar into a slot machine, Lisa was fired for stealing $120 from the register at the deli where she worked. Two days before Christmas, Lisa's mother stepped in and pleaded with the owner to give Lisa another chance. The woman agreed, but that same night Lisa, who had a key to the deli, broke in and stole $180 from the register. She lost it all in the slot machines.

Lisa had hit bottom. She had ruined her family's holiday and sunk to the level of a common thief. "It hit me—what I had done—and it made me sick inside," Lisa says. She knew she needed help. With the encouragement of her parents, Lisa went first to a therapist, and then to Gamblers Anonymous.

To keep the bank from pressing charges that might land their daughter in jail, the Hoffmans covered their daughter's bad checks. They also covered her personal bills, debts on their gas credit card, and therapy costs—amounts that, Lisa estimates, total $10,000.

With the help of Gamblers Anonymous, Lisa began understanding her problem. "Gambling is one of the most addictive things you can do," she says. "There are some people who can handle it, but I can't. I'll never be able to go to a casino again. The first time I do that, I'll be right back where I started."

Lisa, now 20, works as a home health aide and hopes to become an elementary school teacher someday. Looking back on her year as a gambler, she is still stunned by her actions, and she deeply regrets the pain she caused. "It was just one year of my life, but I completely destroyed everything I had worked for," Lisa says. "I have a very supportive and loving family, and I'll never have their complete trust again."

ORGANIZATIONS TO CONTACT

The editors have compiled the following list of organizations concerned with the issues presented in this book. The descriptions are derived from materials provided by the organizations. All have publications or information available for interested readers. The list was compiled on the date of publication of the present volume; the information provided here may change. Be aware that many organizations take several weeks or longer to respond to inquiries, so allow as much time as possible.

American Council on Science and Health (ACSH)
1995 Broadway, 2nd Floor, New York, NY 10023-5860
(212) 362-7044 • fax: (212) 362-4919
website: www.acsh.org

ACSH is a consumer education group composed of physicians, scientists, and policy advisers. It is concerned with educating consumers about health, lifestyle, and environmental issues and the safety of food and pharmaceuticals. The council publishes the quarterly magazine *Priorities* and special reports on the hazards of alcohol and tobacco use.

Americans for Nonsmokers' Rights
2530 San Pablo Ave., Suite J, Berkeley, CA 94702
(510) 841-3032 • fax: (510) 841-3060
e-mail: anr@no-smoke.org • website: www.no-smoke.org

This antismoking organization lobbies local governments to adopt smoke-free indoor air laws. Its educational arm, the American Nonsmokers' Rights Foundation, publishes tobacco education and smoking prevention materials for adolescents, including *The Tobacco Industry Has a Bad Habit* and *How to Butt In! Teens Take Action Guidebook*.

Center for Substance Abuse Prevention (CSAP)
National Clearinghouse for Alcohol and Drug Information (NCADI)
PO Box 2345, Rockville, MD 20847-2345
(800) 729-6686 • fax: (301) 468-6433
e-mail: info@health.org • website: www.health.org

The CSAP leads U.S. government efforts to prevent alcoholism and other substance abuse problems among Americans. Through the NCADI, the center provides the public with a wide variety of information concerning the abuse of alcohol and drugs. Its publications include the bimonthly *Prevention Pipeline*, the booklet *Marijuana: Facts for Teens*, the report "Impaired Driving Among Youth: Trends and Tools for Prevention," brochures, pamphlets, videotapes, and posters.

Drugs and Data Center and Clearinghouse
1600 Research Blvd., Rockville, MD 20850
(800) 732-3277

The clearinghouse distributes the publications of the U.S. Department of Justice, the Drug Enforcement Administration, and other related federal agencies.

Foundation for a Smoke-Free America
PO Box 492028, Los Angeles, CA 90049-8028
(310) 471-4270 • fax: (310) 471-0335
website: www.tobaccofree.org

The foundation is dedicated to educating the public about the dangers of tobacco use. It works to prevent teen smoking through school-based educational initiatives and peer teaching programs. In addition, the foundation produces multimedia presentations for schools and communities and educational videotapes for teens, including *The Truth About Tobacco*.

Institute for Social Research
University of Michigan, 426 Thompson St., Ann Arbor, MI 48104-2321
(734) 764-8354 • fax: (734) 647-4575
e-mail: isr-info@isr.umich.edu • website: www.isr.umich.edu

The institute conducts the annual Monitoring the Future survey, which gathers data on the use of and attitudes toward drugs, alcohol, and tobacco among eighth-, tenth-, and twelfth-grade students. The institute's website includes news releases detailing the findings of the survey.

International Centre for Youth Gambling Problems and High-Risk Behaviors
Faculty of Education, McGill University, 3724 McTavish, Montreal, QC H3A 1Y2 Canada
(514) 398-1391 • fax: (514) 398-3401
e-mail: info@youthgambling.org • website: www.youthgambling.org

The centre researches the causes of youth gambling and participates in the implementation of treatment and prevention programs. The centre's work is published in many academic journals, including the *Journal of Gambling Studies*.

Mothers Against Drunk Driving (MADD)
PO Box 541688, Dallas, TX 75354-1688
(214) 744-6233 • fax: (214) 869-2209
e-mail: info@madd.org • website: www.madd.org

A nationwide grassroots organization, MADD provides support services to victims of drunk driving and attempts to influence policy makers by lobbying for changes in legislation on local, state, and national levels. MADD's public education efforts include its "Rating the States" report, which draws attention to the status of state and federal efforts against drunk driving. MADD publishes the semiannual *Driven* magazine and numerous pamphlets and brochures, including *Straight Talk About Death for Teenagers*.

Narcotics Anonymous (NA)
World Service Office, PO Box 9999, Van Nuys, CA 91409
(818) 773-9999 • fax: (818) 700-0070
website: www.na.org

NA is a twelve-step program that focuses on overcoming the disease of addiction. It publishes *Narcotics Anonymous*, the basic text of the twelve-step process, and numerous pamphlets, such as *Youth and Recovery*.

National Association of State Alcohol and Drug Abuse Directors (NASADAD)
808 17th St. NW, Suite 410, Washington, DC 20006
(202) 293-0090 • fax: (202) 293-1250
e-mail: dcoffice@nasadad.org • website: www.nasadad.org

NASADAD assists the federal and state governments in the development of alcohol and drug abuse prevention and treatment programs throughout the United States. It publishes the newsletter *State Substance Abuse Quarterly* and the annual *State Resources and Services Related to Alcohol and Drug Abuse Problems*.

National Center on Addiction and Substance Abuse at Columbia University (CASA)

633 Third Ave., Floor 19, New York, NY 10017-6706
(212) 841-5200 • fax: (212) 956-8020
e-mail: mnakashi@casacolumbia.org • website: www.casacolumbia.org

CASA is a think tank composed of professionals from many disciplines whose goal is to inform Americans of the economic and social costs of substance abuse. The center conducts research on drug abuse among young people and prevention tactics. It publishes periodic reports, such as "Rethinking Rites of Passage: Substance Abuse on America's Campuses," "Dangerous Liaisons: Substance Abuse and Sex," and "Non-Medical Marijuana: Rite of Passage or Russian Roulette?"

National Clearinghouse for Alcohol and Drug Information

PO Box 2345, Rockville, MD 20847-2345
(800) 729-6686
e-mail: info@health.org • website: www.health.org

The clearinghouse distributes publications of the U.S. Department of Health and Human Services, the National Institute on Drug Abuse, and other federal agencies concerned with alcohol and drug abuse.

National Council on Alcoholism and Drug Dependence (NCADD)

20 Exchange Pl., Suite 2902, New York, NY 10005
(212) 269-7797 • fax: (212) 269-7510
e-mail: national@ncadd.org • website: www.ncadd.org

NCADD is a volunteer health organization that, in addition to helping individuals overcome addictions, advises the federal government on drug and alcohol policies and develops substance abuse prevention and education programs for youth. It publishes fact sheets, such as "Youth and Alcohol," and pamphlets, such as *Who's Got the Power? You . . . or Drugs?*

National Council on Problem Gambling (NCPG)

208 G St. NE, Washington, DC 20002
(202) 547-9204 • fax (202) 547-9206
e-mail: ncpg@ncpgambling.org • website: www.ncpgambling.org

The NCPG was established to spread awareness about the problem of pathological gambling and to ensure the availability of treatment and counseling services to problem gamblers and their families. The council sponsors the publication of the *Journal of Gambling Studies* and publishes brochures and fact sheets, including "Adolescent Gambling and Problem Gambling."

National Criminal Justice Reference Service (NCJRS)

PO Box 6000, Rockville, MD 20849-6000
(800) 851-3420
website: www.ncjrs.org

The NCJRS distributes publications of the U.S. Department of Justice, the National Institute of Justice, and other federal agencies. For a nominal fee, it can provide a bibliography on any topic related to criminal justice, juvenile justice, or substance abuse.

National Institute on Drug Abuse (NIDA)
National Institutes of Health, 6001 Executive Blvd., Rm. 5213, Bethesda, MD 20892
(301) 443-1124
e-mail: information@lists.nida.nih.gov • website: www.nida.nih.gov

NIDA supports and conducts research on drug abuse—including the yearly Monitoring the Future Survey—in order to improve addiction prevention, treatment, and policy efforts. It publishes the bimonthly newsletter *NIDA Notes*, periodic *NIDA Capsules* fact sheets, and a catalog of research reports and public education materials, such as *Marijuana: Facts for Teens*.

BIBLIOGRAPHY

Books

Kellie Anderson	*Young People and Alcohol, Drugs, and Tobacco.* Copenhagen: World Health Organization, 1995.
Brian Castellani	*Pathological Gambling: The Making of a Medical Problem.* Albany: State University of New York Press, 2000.
William L. Fibkins	*What Schools Should Do to Help Kids Stop Smoking.* Larchmont, NY: Eye on Education, 2000.
Michelle Freier, Robert M. Bell, and Phyllis L. Ellickson	*Do Teens Tell the Truth? The Validity of Self-Reported Tobacco Use by Adolescents.* Santa Monica, CA: Rand, 1991.
Thomas J. Glynn	*School Programs to Prevent Smoking: The National Cancer Institute Guide to Strategies That Succeed.* Bethesda, MD: National Institutes of Health, 1994.
Avram Goldstein	*Addiction: From Biology to Drug Policy.* New York: W.H. Freeman, 1994.
Arthur Herscovitz	*Cocaine: The Drug and the Addiction.* Lake Worth, FL: Gardner Press, 1996.
Cynthia Kuhn et al.	*Buzzed: The Straight Facts About the Most Used and Abused Drugs from Alcohol to Ecstasy.* New York: W.W. Norton, 1998.
Mike A. Males	*Smoked: Why Joe Camel Is Still Smiling.* Monroe, ME: Common Courage Press, 1999.
Wendy Mass	*Teen Drug Abuse.* San Diego: Lucent Books, 1998.
William G. McCown	*Best Possible Odds: Contemporary Treatment Strategies for Gambling Disorders.* New York: Wiley, 2000.
Hayley R. Mitchell	*Teen Alcoholism.* San Diego: Lucent Books, 1998.
Donald F. Roberts, Lisa Henriksen, and Peter G. Christenson	*Substance Use in Popular Movies and Music.* Washington, DC: Office of National Drug Control Policy, 1999.
Gail Stewart	*Teen Addicts.* San Diego: Lucent Books, 2000.
Steven Yale Sussman	*Developing School-Based Tobacco Use Prevention and Cessation Programs.* Thousand Oaks, CA: Sage, 1995.
William L. White	*Slaying the Dragon: The History of Addiction Treatment and Recovery in America.* Bloomington, IL: Chestnut Health Systems, 1998.

Periodicals

Alcoholism and Drug Abuse Weekly	"Survey Links Hands-Off Parenting, Teen Drug Use," February 26, 2001. Available from Manisses Communications Group, 208 Governor St., Providence, RI 02906.

Scott Baldauf	"When Parents Are a Part of the Drug Problem," *Christian Science Monitor*, August 28, 2000.
Wendy Bounds	"Keeping Teens from Smoking," *Wall Street Journal*, May 6, 1999.
Jane E. Brody	"Compulsive Gambling: Overlooked Addiction," *New York Times*, May 4, 1999.
Jane E. Brody	"Heading Off a Nation of Teenage Smokers," *New York Times*, November 17, 1998.
Shannon Brownlee and Major Garrett	"Can Pols Really Stop Teens from Smoking?" *U.S. News & World Report*, June 1, 1998.
Angie Cannon and Caroline Kleiner	"Teens Get Real," *U.S. News & World Report*, April 17, 2000.
Christian Century	"Showdown with the Marlboro Man," April 12, 2000.
Christian Science Monitor	"Parenting a Teen," September 23, 1997.
William J. Clinton	"Statement on Efforts to Cut Teen Drug Use," *Weekly Compilation of Presidential Documents*, June 29, 1998. Available from the U.S. Government Printing Office, Superintendent of Documents, PO Box 371954, Pittsburgh, PA 15250-7954.
John Cloud	"Ecstasy Crackdown," *Time*, April 9, 2001.
Matthew Cooper and Elizabeth Roberts	"Trying to Stop a Teen Epidemic," *Newsweek*, April 13, 1998.
Andrew Curry	"In the Mood for a Smoke," *U.S. News & World Report*, October 16, 2000.
Nina G. Dorsch	"Being Real and Being Realistic: Chemical Abuse Prevention, Teen Counselors, and an Ethic of Care," *Journal of Drug Education*, 1997. Available from Baywood Publishing Company, 26 Austin Ave., PO Box 337, Amityville, NY 11701.
Tammerlin Drummond	"Busted for Possession," *Time*, December 7, 1998.
Susan Freinkel, Mark L. Fuerst, and Elizabeth B. Krieger	"Teen Smoking: The Longest Drag," *Health*, July/ August 1999.
Noreen Golfman	"Gambling Addicts," *Canadian Forum*, December 1998. Available from 5502 Atlantic, Halifax, NS B3H 1G4 Canada.
Harper's	"A Safe Haven for Marlboro Kids," December 1997.
Linda Kulman	"Childhood's Little Vices," *U.S. News & World Report*, October 6, 1997.
Marianne Lavelle	"Teen Tobacco Wars," *U.S. News & World Report*, February 7, 2000.
Steven C. Manning	"Teens and Drugs: How Big a Crisis?" *Scholastic Update*, May 2, 1997.

Alexandra Marks	"In-Your-Face Ads Turn Some Kids Off Drugs," *Christian Science Monitor*, August 5, 1999.
Judy Monroe	"The LSD Story," *Current Health 2*, April/May 1998.
Patricia Murphy	"Teen Smokers," *Current Health 2*, November 1999.
Nation's Health	"Teen Drug Use Prevention," April 1997. Available from the American Public Health Association, 800 I St. NW, Washington, DC 20001-3710.
Stephanie Nolen	"All Night, Every Night," *Maclean's*, November 11, 1998.
Gilbert Oskaboose	"Casinos Are for Losers Like Me," *Indian Life*, November/December 1999. Available from Intertribal Christian Communications, 188 Henderson Hwy., Winnipeg, MB R2L 1L6 Canada.
Patrick Perry	"Teen Drug Abuse: Bringing the Message Home," *Saturday Evening Post*, May/June 1998.
Mark Pitsch	"Spreading Out the Blame for Teen Drug Use," *Education Week*, October 9, 1996. Available from Editorial Projects in Education Inc., Suite 100, 6935 Arlington Rd., Bethesda, MD 20814-5233.
Matt Richtel	"The Casino on the Desktop," *New York Times*, March 29, 2001.
Cintra Scott	"Quitting Time," *Scholastic Choices*, February 1999. Available from Scholastic Inc., 2931 E. McCarty St., PO Box 3710, Jefferson City, MO 65102-3710.
Daniel Sneider	"As Teen Drug Use Climbs, Schools Seek New Answers," *Christian Science Monitor*, March 24, 1997.
Jacob Sullum	"Cowboys, Camels, and Kids," *Reason*, April 1998.
Gabriel Trip	"Like Parent, Like Teenager?" *New York Times*, September 15, 1996.
USA Today Magazine	"Teen Ecstasy Use Up, Cocaine and LSD Down," April 2001.
U.S. News & World Report	"Teen Risks," October 7, 1996.
Ned Vizzini	"Teen Angst? Nah!" *New York Times Magazine*, May 17, 1998.
Rick Whitaker	"One Last Chance," *New York Times Magazine*, November 28, 1999.
Working Mother	"Is Your Teen Doing Ecstasy?" December 2000.
Christopher S. Wren	"Teenagers Find Drugs Easy to Obtain and Warnings Easy to Ignore," *New York Times*, October 10, 1996.

INDEX